WITHDRAWN

PRACTICAL SOCIAL WORK

Series Editor: Jo Campling

BASW

Social work is at an important stage in its development. All professions must be responsive to changing social and economic conditions if they are to meet the needs of those they serve. This series focuses on sound practice and the specific contribution which social workers can make to the well-being of our society in the 1980s.

The British Association of Social Workers has always been conscious of its role in setting guidelines for practice and in seeking to raise professional standards. The conception of the Practical Social Work series arose from a survey of BASW members to discover where they, the practitioners in social work, felt there was the most need for new literature. The response was overwhelming and enthusiastic, and the result is a carefully planned, coherent series of books. The emphasis is firmly on practice, set in a theoretical framework. The books will inform, stimulate and promote discussion, thus adding to the further development of skills and high professional standards. All the authors are practitioners and teachers of social work, representing a wide variety of experience.

JO CAMPLING

PRACTICAL SOCIAL WORK

Series Editor: Jo Campling

BASW

PUBLISHED

Social Work and Mental Handicap
David Anderson

Social Work and Mental Illness
Alan Butler and Colin Pritchard

Residential Work
Roger Clough

Social Work with Old People
Mary Marshall

Applied Psychology for Social Workers
Paula Nicolson and Rowan Bayne

Social Work with Disabled People
Michael Oliver

Working in Teams
Malcolm Payne

Adoption and Fostering: Why and How
Carole R. Smith

Social Work with the Dying and Bereaved
Carole R. Smith

Community Work
Alan Twelvetrees

FORTHCOMING

Social Work and Child Abuse
David Ball and David Cooper

The Management and Prevention of Violence
Robert Brown, Stanley Bute and Peter Ford

Welfare Rights Work in the Social Services
Geoff Fimister

Student Supervision in Social Work
Kathy Ford and Alan Jones

Social Work with Computers
Bryan Glastonbury

Working with Families
Gill Gorell Barnes

Social Work with Ethnic Minorities
Alun Jackson

Crisis Intervention in the Social Services
Kieran O'Hagan

Social Care in the Community
Malcolm Payne

Social Work with Juvenile Offenders
David Thorpe, Norman Tutt, David Smith and Christopher Green

Working with Offenders
Hilary Walker and Bill Beaumont (eds)

Adoption and Fostering

Why and How

Carole R. Smith

MACMILLAN

First published 1984 by
Higher and Further Education Division
MACMILLAN PUBLISHERS LTD
London and Basingstoke
Companies and representatives throughout the world

Typeset by
Wessex Typesetters Ltd
Frome, Somerset

Printed in Hong Kong

British Library Cataloguing in Publication Data
Smith, Carole R.
Adoption and fostering.
1. Adoption
I. Title
362.7′34   HV875
ISBN 0–333–35230–0
ISBN 0–333–35231–9 pbk

For Dolores, Bertie and Barry

Any opinions expressed and/or interpretations offered in this book are solely those of
the author and do not necessarily reflect those of any employing authority in the fields
of adoption and fostering.

Contents

1

Adoption in Context and Social Work Intervention

Geographies, said the geographer, are books which, of all books, are most concerned with matters of consequence. They never become old-fashioned. It is very rarely that a mountain changes its position. It is very rarely that an ocean empties itself of its waters. We write of eternal things.

Antoine de Saint-Exupery, *The Little Prince*

Introduction

I doubt that anyone would challenge the view that social workers are concerned with matters of consequence. This assertion is valid across the whole range of social work activities, whether we interpret these as a means of exercising more effective social control or as a way of enhancing the quality of life for individuals and groups within an established political, social and economic structure. At this juncture, however, we are not afforded the continuity of 'eternal things', either in relation to problems which social workers are legitimately expected to confront or with regard to appropriate means of tackling these at a professional and organisational level. We are still faced with questions concerning the interpretation of social problems, the organisation of resources, development of appropriate skills and the identification of potentially successful methods of intervention. Social workers act within the context of political power, ideological debate, economic constraints, changing social and demographic conditions, legally circumscribed choices, as well as responding to professional issues of theory and practice.

Although this book is about social work practice it is with reference to the points above that we must understand the changing significance of adoption in the field of child care. Social work practice essentially involves making decisions and this raises some thorny questions about planning for adoption and working with parents and their children. Such questions concern the conditions under which children should be placed for adoption, which children should be so placed, whether adoption plans should be made without parental agreement, whether and when parental contact should be terminated, and how far we can ensure that adopted children grow up into competent, happy adults. Any discussion of social work practice and adoption must therefore take account of factors which have changed adoption from a minor and uncontentious activity to a central area of concern and often passionate debate.

Which children?

Adoption was legally recognised in 1926. The Report of the Departmental Committee on the Adoption of Children (1972), hereafter referred to as the Houghton Report, defines it as 'the complete severance of the legal relationship between parents and child and the establishment of a new one between the child and his adoptive parents' (p. 4). Although adoption commonly occurred where the adopters were related to, or already knew the child, literature concerned with 'non-relative' adoptions illustrates two particular characteristics of early arrangements. First, children placed for adoption were normally white, healthy babies or toddlers. Ellison, for example, commented in 1958 that *even* a baby with a squint was sometimes wanted and McWhinnie noted in 1967 that 'the concept of the perfect child makes many adoption societies view as unadoptable the child who has the misfortune to have a visible birthmark' (McWhinnie, 1967, p. 26). Writing in 1947, Lockridge made similar comments about practice in the United States. Secondly, prospective adopters tended to be viewed as generous public-spirited citizens whose wish to adopt amply suited them for the job. In 1970 Bowerbank remarked that case papers of adoption societies operating during and following the last war suggest a concern, not with the suitability of adoptive applicants, but with the sex, colouring and characteristics of the babies which they were prepared to accept. Emphasis was commonly placed on meeting the social and emotional needs of childless couples. Similar attitudes coloured adoption practice in the United States. The Florida Adoption Act of 1943, for example, was bitterly fought because of requirements for social investigation and supervision of prospective adopters (see Witmer *et al.*, 1963).

There has, however, been a dramatic change in this picture of adoption. Arrangements made by voluntary societies and local authorities are now governed by the Adoption Agencies Regulations,

1976. These Regulations were first introduced in 1939 in an effort to improve practice and are, at present, under review by the DHSS. Social workers have become more sophisticated in their expectations of professional competence and this has clearly influenced their approach to work in adoption. A major change has also occurred in the diminishing number of babies being relinquished for adoption and in our knowledge about the kinds of children who may benefit from this sort of placement. Many practitioners and researchers have noted a decline in adoption placements of babies since the late 1960s and evidence suggests that greater availability of abortion, effective contraception and more flexible social attitudes to illegitimacy and single-parent families, have contributed to a change in surrendering patterns (see Lambert, 1971; Triseliotis and Lobban, 1973; Tizard, 1977). While the above trends were becoming apparent, social workers were beginning to focus attention on those children with 'special needs' who required permanent substitute families.

Several important factors encouraged this change in emphasis. First, research in Britain and the United States showed that not only could families be found to adopt older, black and mixed race children but that such placements also had a very good chance of turning out well. In the United States, Kadushin (1970a) reported on a follow-up study of children aged between five and twelve years at placement. Fanshel (1972), Grow and Shapiro (1974), and in Britain, Gill and Jackson (1983), have considered the outcome of transracial adoptions. Secondly, during a review of research Clarke (1981) comments that results 'give us cause for cautious optimism' about the developmental progress of children from deprived and disrupted backgrounds who are subsequently placed with adoptive families. Thirdly, it was becoming apparent that leaving young children in residential care to see 'how they would develop' or attempting to assess their potential by early psychological and intelligence testing, failed to provide any guarantees to prospective adopters and sometimes hindered normal development (see Wittenborn, 1957; Rutter, 1970). Fourthly, Rowe and Lambert's blockbuster, *Children who Wait* (1973), brought social workers face to face with the facts about many children who were in danger of growing up in care. Translating their research findings into national terms, Rowe and Lambert suggested that there were about 7,000 children waiting for family placement. The authors comment that, 'all those who worked on this project found it a sobering experience . . . the findings are depressing, not so much because there is anything new or startling about them, but because so many of the old problems are still with us' (Rowe and Lambert, 1973, p. 99). Fifthly, some widely publicised 'tug of love' cases between foster and biological parents focused attention on the legal insecurity of fostering arrangements and suggested that adoption would better serve the welfare of children who could not return to their own families within the foreseeable future.

In varying degrees the five factors outlined above prompted the development of adoption services for a whole range of children with special needs. At the same time family resources were being developed in a more precise and adventurous way through 'specialist' or 'professional' schemes to meet the needs of severely handicapped children, disturbed or delinquent adolescents, or adults requiring some form of community support. Local authorities and voluntary societies have been energetic in attempting to maximise the chances of family placement through organising regional resource exchanges, setting up 'adoption shops', using publicity, arranging adoption parties, amongst many initiatives which are seen as vital by the converted and sometimes condemned as damaging and inappropriate by the more cautious. A similar 'drive towards adoption' has also occurred in the United States, exemplified by such publications as *No Child is Unadoptable* (Churchill *et al.*, 1979). Adoption has undergone a major revolution since the 1960s and is now seen as a real alternative for children regardless of their personal or family characteristics. This, however, is only one part of the story. We must examine changes in professional attitudes and legal developments before we are able to grasp the whole picture.

Which plan?

At the time of writing, a furore has erupted over what has been termed by some 'aggressive' planning for children in care, terminating parental contact where rehabilitation cannot be quickly effected and decisions to place children for adoption without parental agreement, rather than choosing the more open-ended alternative of long-term fostering. Having reached the point where many children may realistically be placed for adoption, we are now faced with questions about the desirability of planning and decision-making which this may entail. It is tempting to accept this kind of dilemma as 'a given' in social work and to go about our business while the conflict rages on. In my view, however, we cannot adequately discuss adoption practice without some reference to the social, legal and ideological context in which practitioners make their decisions.

The law relating to adoption has always allowed that, under certain conditions, adoption orders may be granted without parental agreement. However, the Houghton Report, the 1975 Children Act and the consolidating 1980 Child Care Act did much more than just amend and extend previous legislation along the same lines. The 1975 Children Act, following the Houghton Report's recommendations, *qualitatively* changed the place of adoption in child care policy and practice by recognising its significance for a wide range of children, establishing it as an important alternative for children in care, and facilitating planning towards this end. The Houghton Report and subsequent legislation also recognised the significance for children of a lapse of time and provided legal safeguards against sudden and unplanned disruptions of caring relationships which may have developed outside a child's biological family.

Changes in the law have reflected a growing concern with planning for children in long-term care. In 1971 Parker suggested that, collectively, social workers were failing to plan adequately on behalf of such children. Rowe and Lambert (1973) pointed out that of the 2,812 children in their study, 61 per cent were expected to remain in care until they were eighteen years old. Adcock (1980a) and the Houghton Report similarly present evidence that an alarming number of children seem likely to grow up in care. This issue is obviously not something which we have just discovered and Packman (1975) provides a historical analysis of how this question has been tackled over the years. She refers to the approach of some local authorities in the 1950s which 'would delight recent critics of long term care for children who deplore the lack of decisiveness and tendency to drift in much current child care practice' (Packman, 1975, p. 34). However, some would argue that an emphasis on early decision-making may lead to ill-considered and inappropriate action, political expediency and a neglect of the rights of biological parents, in our haste to make adoption plans for their children. Goldstein *et al.* (1973 and 1980), for example, outraged many social workers by suggesting that once a child's caretaker (foster parent) had become his psychological parent and previous ties to biological parents had significantly weakened, the placement should be made permanent by means of adoption. While recognising that older children are more able and more likely to maintain psychological ties with absent parents and that these should not be disrupted, Goldstein *et al.* suggested that younger children are unable to sustain relationships in the absence of rewarding interaction and that given the passage of time 'it would be unreasonable to presume that a child's residual ties with his absent parents are more significant than those which have developed between him and his longtime caretakers' (Goldstein *et al.*, 1980, p. 46).

Lothian seems to have been one of the first local authorities to consider policy and practice in the light of Goldstein *et al.*'s emphasis on time limits, psychological ties and legally safeguarding the permanence of placements (see McKay, 1980). More recently Hussell and Monaghan (1982) have reported on policy changes in Lambeth which reflect this philosophy. Permanence is viewed as 'the most important ingredient in good child care practice' and the policy requires that children entering care under the age of ten should not remain in care for longer than two years. The alternatives to care are seen as either rehabilitation or permanent placement with substitute families, the second option often involving termination of parental contact and adoption. Long-term fostering is clearly differentiated from permanent placement and is only chosen under particular circumstances which must be argued in terms of the child's welfare.

Those who support the principle of early planning and decision-making argue that this approach must derive from vigorous attempts to achieve rehabilitation, a recognition of parental rights, and a commitment to involving parents in discussions about their children's future. Hussell and Monaghan emphasise these points, asserting that Lambeth's policy is 'primarily and crucially . . . about stopping children slipping into long term care. It is therefore as much to do with good quality imaginative prevention and rehabilitation work as with permanent separation. It is not the operation of an adoption mafia nor is it a management tool for saving money' (Hussell and Monaghan, 1982, p. 7). There are certainly other local authorities in Britain which have either accepted comparable policies or are working towards this position. In the United States social workers have been grappling with similar dilemmas. Two programmes, the Almeda Project in California and Special Emphasis for Early Return, concentrate on speedy decision-making through using contracts, time-limited goals, explanations and support for parents, and, if rehabilitation cannot be effected quickly, permanent placement with substitute families.

It is against this backcloth that the furore has erupted, exemplified by such headlines as 'Captive Families: When Parents Lose their Children' (*New Society*, 27/5/82); 'Child Care in Crisis' (*The Guardian*, 3/11/82); and 'Contrary to Natural Justice' (*Community Care*, 29/7/82). Some commentators, notably Robert Holman, have argued that the 1975 Children Act represents a backlash against the proper recognition of parental rights and that it has influenced social work practice towards 'rescuing' children from their families, planning their future without reference to parents and too easily neglecting efforts to promote prevention and rehabilitation. The elements of this debate are complex and difficult to disentangle because competing arguments continually shift between different levels of analysis covering professional practice, social structure, legal constraints, economic and class variables, the allocation of power and resources, politically governed choices and ideologically based demands for social change. Fox (1982) attempts to outline the important areas of disagreement between those who support early decision-making and emphasise the place of adoption in planning for children in care, and those who take a critical attitude towards this approach and question the political and social structure on which it is based.

It would be easy to conclude that the 'permanency debate' is really about the quality of social work practice and the use of resources. However, there remain inescapable difficulties regarding the balance between parents' rights and children's needs, the weight which should be given to biological relatedness, the best way of safeguarding and promoting the welfare of children and the acceptability of present legislation. These issues are concerned not only with professional competence and compassion but with the political structure and ideological values which inform social work practice. This book must therefore tackle two related questions: first, under what conditions should social workers consider planning for adoption, and secondly, how can they work in such a way as to enhance the probability of a successful outcome to adoption arrangements?

Social workers and adoption

Adoption, and indeed fostering, present social workers with somewhat different problems from those which they usually face in helping people who cannot cope adequately with the demands of everyday life. How do we work with prospective foster or adoptive parents and what are we trying to achieve? What kind of relationship should we have with them? Are they like other groups of clients and if not how are they different? What kind of information and how much should we share with them? Are there particular skills or techniques which we should use? Is there any research which can help us to do the job better? Or, more generally, do we actually have anything to contribute, or could they manage just as well without us? I refer here to fostering as well as adoption because much that follows will be relevant to both activities, particularly where foster placements are intended to be permanent or become so through the passage of time.

In making this comment I do not intend to blur the differences between adoption and fostering or to prejudge the argument that long-term or permanent placements should be intentionally planned and should *only* involve boarding out as a purposefully designed settling-in period prior to adoption.

Before the 1926 Adoption Act arrangements were made without the benefit of any legal framework and resulted in quasi-adoptive situations or 'de facto' adoptions. For many years parents have been free to place their children for adoption with whomsoever they wished and without the intervention of adoption agencies or social work services. Grey and Blunden's (1971) statistical survey covered a sample of 3,400 adoption applications made to 138 courts in Great Britain. In 29 per cent of cases the placements had been arranged directly between parents and prospective adopters or through third parties. The Houghton Committee was concerned about the number of children who were being placed for adoption without recourse to social work help. Despite divided evidence on this matter, the Committee recommended that adoption placements made independently of an agency should become illegal unless a child was related to the prospective adopters (as defined by the 1958 Adoption Act). This recommendation was incorporated into the 1975 Children Act and has now been implemented. In reaching its conclusions the Houghton Committee stated that, 'the decision to place a child with a particular couple is the most important stage in the adoption process. Adoption law must give assurance of adequate safeguards for the welfare of the child at this stage. This assurance rests mainly upon the skilled work of the adoption services, which includes preparation for adoptive parenthood' (p. 23). Later, the Committee's report refers to the increasing professional skills and knowledge of agency social workers. Given this vote of confidence in social work expertise, it behoves us to be clear about why we should intervene in adoption arrangements and how we can help to achieve successful results.

The nature of difference

Most parents bring up their children without social work interference. The suggestion that social workers must be involved in adoption arrangements rests on the assumption that adoption is significantly different and presents particular difficulties which are not found in non-adoptive families. Kellmer-Pringle points out that 'perhaps the biggest of all the fallacies is the assumption that to adopt is little different from having children of one's own. In many respects, which may or may not prove to be important, it is manifestly different' (Kellmer-Pringle, 1967, p. 25). A vast, and growing number of research studies have attempted to assess the nature of difference and its impact on adoption outcome. Difficulties, particularly those deriving from adoption, may be faced by childless couples in coping with infertility and parenting 'someone else's' child: problems of child development relating to stress before, during or after birth; emotional conflicts associated with the socially contrived nature of adoption; the minority status of adoptive families and explanations to adopted children. The empirical observation of such difficulties and their influence on adoption outcome will be considered in Chapter 2.

It may be argued that David Kirk has provided the single most detailed analysis of the unique and delicate nature of the adoptive relationship in his book, *Shared Fate* (1964). Adoptive parents, according to Kirk, are faced with several dilemmas. These he defines as first, 'enchantment versus disenchantment'. Are they going to pretend that they are just like any other parents or will they acknowledge their peculiar status? Secondly, 'integration versus differentiation'. Are they going to differentiate the child from others by 'telling' and talking about adoption or will they forgo such reminders in favour of integration? Thirdly, 'ignorance versus knowledge of the child's background'. Do they forget what they have been told about the child's background in an effort to deny that it is different from their own, or do they incorporate it into family conversation and face the reality of adoption? Fourthly, 'reproductive morals versus the principle of respect for individual personality'. How do they tell an adopted child about his illegitimate birth (or in the case of older children about parental inadequacy, illness or rejection) without passing a negative judgement on biological parents? Kirk suggests that these dilemmas do not form part of the 'cultural script' for parenthood, and thus compound the role handicap of adoptive parents. They represent the difficulties which are inherent in fulfilling the role demands of adoptive parenthood. Patterns of managing these dilemmas, suggests Kirk, may be broadly divided into 'acknowledgement of difference' and 'rejection of difference'. The latter pattern may be illustrated by an inability to handle questions from others about adoption or a child's background, an emphasis on matching and 'natural' spacing of adopted children within the family, lessening the impact of 'telling', devaluing the importance of historical information, emphasising the part played by fate or 'divine intervention', or simply forgetting that the child was born to other parents. 'Acknowledgement of difference' is shown by a desire for some kind of ritual to mark the status of adoptive parenthood, a willingness to eschew matching, announcing the adoption publicly, visiting other adoptive parents, celebrating adoption anniversaries, and acknowledging common problems with other adopters.

Kirk suggests that harmonious and satisfying parent–child relationships, family stability, and permanence of the family as a group, require adoptive parents to achieve an attitude based on 'acknowledgement of difference' and in association with this, open communication about adoption. It should be noted that Kirk did not demonstrate an empirical relationship between acknowledgement of difference, communication and successful outcome in terms of a happier, more satisfying, or qualitatively better family environment for adopted children – he merely hypothesised that this relationship existed. His insistence on equating 'rejection of difference' with poor communication, denial of adoption and less favourable outcome is also somewhat simplistic and open to criticism on the grounds of research design and interpretation of data. Subsequent research findings also question the validity of Kirk's model and it's implications for practice. I will return to this point in the last chapter.

What kind of intervention?

I have already commented on the somewhat 'easy-going' approach to adoption placements which was evident in early practice. With regard to matching physical, intellectual and social characteristics of babies, their biological parents and prospective adopters, however, great care was taken to ensure an acceptable and appropriate similarity as far as was practically possible. It may be argued that conscientious matching went hand in hand with a failure to help adopters recognise their 'role handicap'. For example, Thunen writing in 1958 suggested that 'there is no essential difference in the long run between parenthood by adoption and parenthood by the biological process . . . these people are parents first and foremost, parents by virtue of a relationship that has grown and is continuing to grow, not by virtue of the particular way their child came into their lives' (Thunen, 1958, p. 11). This kind of attitude is vigorously opposed by Kirk who suggests that it 'sanctions the adoptive parents' desire to slough off their self-image as atypical parents, to move from acknowledgement of difference to rejection of difference' (Kirk, 1964, p. 149). Gradually, social workers were becoming more sophisticated in their approach to adoption and their grasp of psychodynamic processes. This, together with increasing knowledge of factors which might influence parent–child relationships, and thus the quality of adoption outcome, combined to support changing attitudes to the acceptability of prospective adopters. Rowe questioned the assumption that adoption applicants were always just 'worthy citizens' and notes that 'conviction about the need and justification for studying the personalities and motives of prospective adopters has grown with professional knowledge and confidence' (Rowe, 1966, p. 153). We must remember also, that as the number of babies relinquished for adoption declined, agencies had a much greater choice of prospective adopters and could select the 'best candidates'.

These factors tended to shift the emphasis to assessment and selection of adoption applicants. It is well recognised that appropriate selection is a difficult task and various aids have been suggested to complement social work skills. For example, Kuhlmann and Robinson (1951) explored the use of Rorschach Tests, Adrian *et al.* (1966) considered other psychological tests such as the Minnesota Multiphasic Personality Inventory, and Edwards (1975) suggested the application of self-administered questionnaires to identify psychiatric or emotional disturbance in prospective adopters. It would appear that the age of science had dawned on social work practice! In the main, however, it continued to be social work knowledge and interviewing skills which were used to assess applicants' ability to cope with infertility, degree of maturity and flexibility, attitudes to biological parents, illegitimacy, talking to children about adoption, parenting capabilities, and so on. The literature commonly uses terms like 'interrogation', 'investigation', 'vetting', and refers to the need for 'psychological screening' in order to 'eliminate' those who are incapable of successful adoptive parenthood. Areas to be investigated as a basis for assessment are set out by the Advisory Council on Child Care (1970), and in the United States guidance is provided by the Child Welfare League of America's Standards for Adoption Service. Similar factors informing the assessment of foster parents are included in the report of the Working Party on Fostering Practice (1976).

Despite the professional appeal of rigorous assessment and selection, its place in fostering and adoption practice has been challenged on a number of grounds. First, Triseliotis (1970) has suggested that even if adequate assessment depended only on interviewing time, detailed exploration of significant areas would be beyond the resources of agencies and social workers. Secondly, if applicants and social workers view assessment and selection as the focus of their interaction, it seems probable that the former will do their best to make a favourable impression and will learn little about the tasks of adoptive parenthood. Thirdly, while it may be relatively easy to recognise grossly unsuitable or disturbed applicants, questions have been raised about the sophistication of social workers' diagnostic skills and their ability to assess the suitability of applicants within the broad range of 'normal' motivation and social and emotional adjustment. Fourthly, the assumption that we know which characteristics to look for in potentially successful adoption placements is not borne out by research, least of all in relation to prospective adoptive parents. Follow-up studies have indicated that the mere clustering of particular qualities or characteristics does not ensure a successful outcome to adoption arrangements. What does seem to influence adoption outcome is the way in which these discrete elements are combined to provide a total pattern of family functioning; home atmosphere, parent–child interaction, happy, satisfying and accepting family relationships. Fifthly, it has been argued that assessment is inappropriate to the placement of children with special needs. What is required is not assessment and selection, but education and preparation for parenting older or handicapped children and those from different racial backgrounds.

Kellmer-Pringle and some of her colleagues have consistently challenged social workers' concern with assessment. I think we should take their comments seriously when they remark, 'there are few generally accepted assessment techniques for determining who will make a good or bad parent, or clear cut predictors of potential for successful parenthood. Why then do we argue, and indeed act, as if these questions had definite or absolute answers where adoptive parents are concerned?' (Seglow *et al.*, 1972, p. 171). If there is little evidence to suggest which kinds of people will make 'good' or 'bad' adoptive parents, there is a danger that social workers will substitute their own ideas about desirable qualities and characteristics. Triseliotis suggests that this was the case in the agencies which he studied and that criteria for selection often 'represented the views, principles, personal beliefs and prejudices of individual workers or committees' (Triseliotis, 1970). I am sure that we have all heard social workers refer to experience, intuition, feeling, gut-reaction, as playing some, if not a major part, in their assessment of prospective adoptive and foster parents.

A concern about the negative aspects of assessment and selection has led some social workers to support an approach based on preparation and education. Literature describing practice in the United States has provided a push in this direction and has been taken up and published by British Agencies for Adoption and Fostering and the National Foster Care Association. Specialist agencies which concentrate on placing older and handicapped children have also developed practice and procedures which emphasise preparation, education, and continuing support for families and children placed with them. However, I refer above to 'some social workers' because it is apparent that assessment is still the guiding principle in much adoption and fostering practice. This may be appreciated from the approach, method of working, interaction with applicants, and the procedural framework of agencies which militate against working effectively in this way.

It must also be recognised that a focus on preparation and education necessitates a reappraisal of our professional self-image and our relationship with applicants. I suspect that this presents difficulties for many social workers who consciously or unconsciously like the idea of a professional mystique which depends on holding specialist knowledge and skills in diagnosis, assessment, and treatment; knowledge and skills which are not open to or understood by laymen who may only have compassion and concern to guide them. If social workers approach prospective foster and adoptive parents on this basis there is a danger that interaction will reflect a professional worker–client relationship, which defines the worker's interpretations and values as more valid than the client's and confronts the latter's problems rather than exploring his strengths. I do not wish to oversimplify this matter or to suggest that we might as well all go home. However, we are interested here in how social workers can constructively work with prospective adopters and foster parents and, in relation to this, what knowledge and skills we may have to offer.

How then does preparation and education differ from assessment and selection? The object of the former approach is both to prepare applicants for adoptive parenthood and to help *them* decide whether they are willing and able to cope with the additional tasks which this will involve. This change in emphasis also presupposes that the relationship between social workers and applicants will shift from that of assessor and assessed, with its associated problems of inhibiting open and honest communication, to one which brings together co-operating individuals working jointly towards a better understanding of adoption and preparing for the particular tasks and attitudes which the adoptive relationship entails. Hagen, writing in the United States asserts that 'the worker's role is on a peer basis working with applicants towards placement, not on a worker–client basis, attempting to determine if they should get a child' (Hagen, 1972, p. 6).

I have already referred to Kirk's views about the 'role handicap' suffered by adoptive parents. In 1967 and 1969 he explained his ideas at conferences held in Britain and asserted that 'adoptive parents confront a series of difficulties that are not shared by natural parents; secondly, that adopters are not prepared for these difficulties either by guidelines in the culture generally or by the professional groups that mean to assist in adoption; thirdly that without such preparation for their role, adopters face unnecessary strains in their relationships with their children' (Kirk, 1970, p. 108). Kirk's argument about the nature of adoptive relationships thus demands that assessment and selection should be discarded in favour of an approach which prepares prospective adopters for their distinctive role. The assessment model is based on the premise that adoption applicants either have or do not have the necessary characteristics and qualities to make successful adoptive parents and that skilled social work investigation can select those who have whatever it is we are looking for, to a sufficient degree, to pass the test. *The social worker makes the choice*.

Preparation and education, however, presuppose that prospective adopters have the capacity to understand the tasks essential to adoptive parenthood, can be helped to anticipate how they will deal with these, can learn alternative methods of communication and handling problems, are able to develop strengths and personal skills, and know themselves well enough to assess their own expectations and needs. *The social worker helps the applicant to make the choice*. An assessment model also suggests that once applicants are accepted as prospective adopters, they have, by definition 'got what it takes' to do the job. Intensive social work involvement is limited to the pre-acceptance period of investigation. However, a preparation model asserts that applicants can only be prepared to a relatively incomplete degree during the initial phase and that learning continues throughout introductions to a child and subsequent placement. Social work help is essential following placement, when prospective adopters come face to face with their own feelings and reactions, changing attitudes of those around them, and the child's demands and responses to moving in. Frequent support and advice are necessary when babies are placed for adoption and are absolutely vital when older children are joining new families. Such an approach demands that social workers enable the development of an open and trusting relationship with prospective adopters, so that the latter can ask for help without fear that they will be considered inadequate, incapable or stupid.

Group discussion

An emphasis on preparation and education has led to the development of group discussions as an important part of the procedure. It has been suggested that adoption and fostering applicants may feel more relaxed in discussing their feelings and ideas with others in a similar situation, that they may be more responsive to interpretations and suggestions from their peers, that they may become more flexible about the kinds of children they could accept, and that they are more willing to use a social worker as 'enabler' or 'facilitator' in a group setting. In the United States the use of groups has become well established as a major component of the adoption process, both before and after placement. Practice in Britain has similarly seen some shift from an emphasis on individual interviews to group discussions. The National Foster Care Association considered the educational opportunities which could be provided through the medium of groups to be so important that this organisation, in association with Barnardo's, imported and subsequently modified a training package from the United States. This package includes films, tapes, exercises, role-play, and a host of imaginative ways for adults to anticipate and learn to deal with problems which they may face when children are placed with their families. 'Parenting Plus' training groups have become a well-known part of British fostering practice, and have now been extended to cover course content for those who intend to foster adolescents. The approach and much of the content of 'Parenting Plus' sessions are equally relevant to preparing prospective adoptive parents.

What do we know about working with adoption applicants?

Most social workers are likely to have some idea about how they would approach the task of working with prospective adopters. We seem to take little notice, however, of what happens at the 'receiving end'. Relatively few researchers and practitioners have attempted to find out how social work help is perceived and assessed by clients, if it is acceptable, and whether what we say and do has the intended effect. The same is true for adoption practice, where most research has concentrated on measuring long-term outcome rather than on evaluating what happens before and after children are placed. However, we do have a few clues. In the United States, Gochros (1967) discovered that prospective adopters of children already in placement saw themselves as being 'on probation' and did not perceive their social workers as supportive or helpful. My own research (1980) indicated that social workers were largely concerned with assessment and evaluation of adoption applicants. Not surprisingly the prospective adopters saw their interviews with agency workers in the same light. Well over half of the eighty-five couples in my sample said that they had been worried about expressing their ideas spontaineously and had been anxious to make a good impression. Again and again respondents made comments like:

> We were putting on an act if you like. We knew what they wanted and we were so afraid of not being accepted that we weren't prepared to be forthright with them and tell them what we did think. We had to hold ourselves back many a time.

> You don't know what to expect. You are self-conscious all the time, trying not to slip up. You kind of feel they want to trip you up, and you think if you say the wrong thing you will endanger your chances.

> Its just another procedure you have to get through. I would do anything so long as I can adopt – if they told me to stand on my head, I would do.

Only sixteen respondents felt that they had been helped to think more clearly about adoption or had developed their understanding of adoptive parenthood. These responses were so similar across so many different agencies and social workers that it is difficult to explain them by reference to individual problems. It seems much more likely that common social work techniques and procedural frameworks were operating throughout the adoption process.

Despite a growing emphasis on group discussion, there is similarly little research evidence to help us evaluate this method of education. In the United States, Wiehe (1976) considered the degree of attitude change concerning infertility, unmarried parents, and telling children about their adoption in three groups of prospective adopters before and after several contacts with the agency. One group underwent a number of individual diagnostic interviews with a social worker, the second took part in group discussions with other applicants, and the third (control group) was not exposed to any form of adoption study. Wiehe concludes that members of the first two groups all showed some attitudinal change in the areas mentioned and all perceived the procedure as 'moderately evaluative'. However, those prospective adopters who took part in group discussions displayed a significant difference from others in their perception of the procedure as constituting *preparation* for adoptive parenthood. Group members were able to share knowledge and ideas and were 'apparently able to use each other to test and expand their views'. Prospective adopters said that this had been helpful in enabling them to clarify attitudes and feelings. Respondents to my own research made similar points and these are reinforced in studies by Reeves and Dolan (1978) and Kerrane *et al.* (1980).

Conclusion

I have considered a variety of approaches to working with adoption applicants summarised by Richards (1970) as the 'slap happy' method, 'careful investigation by a trained adoption worker', the 'scientific approach', and lastly, the 'modern method' which depends on 'educative group techniques where all who want to adopt join discussion groups and those who are unsuitable eliminate themselves' (Richards, 1970, p. 68). There is no research evidence which would help us choose between these approaches in terms of relative outcome. However, for the purpose of this book I will have to make a choice which must be based on experience, common sense, a realistic appraisal of social work skills and the limited research findings at our disposal. For the reasons outlined in this chapter I will concentrate on preparation and education for foster and adoptive parenthood. This, of course, is only one part of the equation; we must also consider decision-making and working with children and their biological parents.

Before closing this chapter a note of warning should be sounded. There is no suggestion from supporters of the preparation model, that assessment can, or should, be totally ignored. As Wiehe points out, 'the agency is given responsibility by the court to pick suitable adoptive parents for children available for adoption. This reality naturally introduces the element of evaluation. While the element of evaluation cannot be avoided it need not become, however, the focus of the study' (Wiehe, 1976, p. 135). How social workers handle the question of assessment will vary according to which approach they choose, as will become clear when we take a detailed look at practice. This chapter has been concerned to outline the context of adoption practice and the principles which will inform the 'nuts and bolts' of intervention. We may now move on to assess the knowledge which is available to help us make decisions and to facilitate a satisfactory outcome for adoptive families.

2

Is Blood Thicker than Water?

> To me, you are still nothing more than a little boy who is just like a
> hundred thousand other little boys. And I have no need of you. And you,
> on your part, have no need of me. To you, I am nothing more than a fox
> like a hundred thousand other foxes. But if you tame me, then we shall
> need each other. To me, you will be unique in all the world. To you, I
> shall be unique in all the world.
>
> Antoine de Saint-Exupery, *The Little Prince*

Introduction

Adoption is one of those subjects about which social workers hold
some strong views. I have met social workers who 'do not agree' with
adoption because they think it is 'too final, too risky', or they have
come across an adoptive family with problems or met an adopted
youngster from an unhappy placement. Others may point to the
socially contrived nature of adoption and assert that this is bound, of
necessity, to cause all kinds of relationship and identity problems for
children and parenting dilemmas for adults. These opinions are
rarely based on what research has to tell us about the subject and
more frequently reflect a mixture of personal values, anxiety,
ignorance, and sometimes fear about making that final decision to
substitute social relationships for biological ties. Such feelings and
attitudes become even more powerful when we talk about placing
children with special needs and when this further involves termination of parental contact or dispensation of parents' agreement.

If adoption is to be considered as one alternative for children who
cannot return to live with their own families, then social workers must
take a critical look at their own reactions to this possibility. Clearly
they will not get very far in this exercise unless they have the benefit of
research findings; that is, of accumulated knowledge in this field. To
eschew research in favour of personal feelings and attitudes is simply
not acceptable. Knowledge is one element which distinguishes
professional workers from lay helpers, and which enables us, when

challenged, to argue the case for making particular decisions. Of course, experience adds to our store of knowledge, but it must be recognised that experience can only be a personal and partial source of information. Professional competence and identity depends on having knowledge about those factors which significantly influence social behaviour and which by having general explanatory value, inform our understanding of, and approach to, specific difficulties and individual distress.

Follow-up studies of adoption outcome

Follow-up research designs have enjoyed considerable popularity in the United States and Britain and there is thus a burgeoning amount of information at our disposal. Such studies have concentrated on children placed at various ages with their adoptive families, from different racial backgrounds and with a range of pre-placement experiences. Evaluation of outcome has been attempted at different stages of childhood and young adulthood. It is impossible to do justice here to the variations in research design or to the complexities of data collection, analysis and interpretation. It is possible, however, to point out some trends in research findings and to identify those areas which require additional investigation.

Most follow-up studies have classified outcome on a number of dimensions. Despite the kind of rigorous testing and evaluation to which non-adoptive families would rarely be subjected, research in both Britain and the United States generally identifies 'successful' outcome in *at least* 75 per cent of cases. Kadushin's work is of particular interest as the children in his study joined their new families when they were between five and twelve years old and had a mean age of nearly fourteen years when outcome was assessed. These children had previously lived in socially deprived conditions, frequently suffered physical neglect and had parents who presented a picture of 'considerable personal pathology compounded of promiscuity, mental deficiency, alcoholism, imprisonment and psychosis' (Kadushin, 1970a, p. 207). It is noteworthy that Kadushin was able to report satisfactory follow-up results for between 82 and 87 per cent of children, depending on the specific outcome measure used.

Researchers have also related child and parent characteristics to outcome in an attempt to identify significant variables. In most cases they have not been able to demonstrate an association between a child's age, number of previous moves and the quality of outcome. However, the majority of children were placed with their adoptive families at a young age and without having experienced severe disruption. Witmer *et al.*, Ripple, Hoopes, and Kadushin did establish a connection between age-related factors and outcome, and Bohman measured a tendency towards greater maladjustment in those children who had spent longer periods in residential care prior to placement. Attempts to identify important characteristics of adoptive parents and families have yielded rather inconsistent results. Easily measured variables such as age of adopters and duration of marriage appear to be relatively unimportant, except where they become significant in terms of flexibility, energy and enjoyment of parenting activities – a finding which we might expect to apply in most families. Previous experience of parenting and the existence or addition of other children to the family again seem to be less important than parental attitudes and the adopted child's perception of being fully accepted and integrated into family life.

Research findings with regard to the socio-economic status of adoptive parents continue to be conflicting and rather baffling. Any association between this variable and outcome appears to be related to more subtle aspects of parental attitudes and expectations, communication patterns, family lifestyle, and so on. Hoopes *et al*. did note a relationship between parental pressure for academic achievement and children's negative attitude towards school and poorer overall adjustment, factors which may be associated with higher socio-economic status. Fanshel comments that we still know little about the qualitative nature of a relationship between socio-economic groupings and outcome and that 'rather than the topic being closed out by definitive findings, it is only at the stage where intriguing questions are being raised and where further research would be very useful' (Fanshel, 1972, p. 329). Some researchers have demonstrated a relationship between aspects of infertility and outcome although quantifying responses and feelings in this area is a complex business. Lawder *et al*. and Grow and Shapiro's findings suggest that infertility is not, in itself, a negative factor and that a willingness to talk about this subject and an enthusiastic acceptance of adoption are indicative of successful outcome.

What seems to have most surprised researchers is the lack of a significant association between quantifiable aspects of telling and talking about adoption and the nature of outcome. The absence of a clearly defined relationship has been replicated in studies by Wittenborn, Ripple, Jaffee and Fanshel, Kornitzer and Raynor. Although it is recognised that children may be distressed if they learn about their status from people other than their adoptive parents, research findings have raised questions about the assumption that this topic is of central importance for the well-being of adopted children. Reporting on their work in the United States, Jaffee and Fanshel remark that 'we learned with some surprise that only a single aspect of revelation was definitely associated with the nature of the adoptive outcome'. This concerned those adoptees who showed a strong curiosity about their past and wanted to know more than their adoptive parents were willing or able to tell them. In these cases, adoptees tended to manifest a more problematic adjustment in a variety of life–space areas. However, 'none of the other ostensibly important aspects of the telling – the timing of the initial revelation, the nature and amount of material revealed, or the frequency of subsequent allusion to adoption – were appreciably correlated with outcome' (Jaffee and Fanshel, 1970, p. 313). Raynor reached similar conclusions from her British follow-up study of adult adoptees and their families. The satisfaction of adoptees was closely related to their contentment with information about their background and the ease which they felt in approaching their adoptive parents about this subject. This association was also found to influence the extent to which adoptees had achieved a successful life adjustment.

However, satisfaction with the adoptive experience and classification of adjustment was *not* related to the amount of information imparted or the frequency with which the matter was discussed. While it was important for successful life adjustment that parents had explained adoption to their children, the timing of this revelation was less significant than the way in which children learned about their adoptive status. Rather like Kornitzer, Raynor concludes that specific aspects of telling and talking about adoption, such as timing and frequency of discussion and the amount of information imparted, are less predictive of outcome than 'the feelings behind the communication'.

Common sense would indicate there is likely to be a fine balance between the desirability of accepting and talking about a child's adoptive status and helping a child to feel integrated and wanted as a member of the adoptive family. Kadushin focuses on this point when he says that 'outcome was positively related to the parents' acceptance of the child, to their perception of him as a member of the family, and negatively related to self-consciousness by parents regarding adoptive status' (Kadushin, 1970a, p. 210). It would seem that adoptive parents who view their children as 'different' and who emphasise this by repeated references to adoptive status and discussions about background are *not* more likely to achieve a successful outcome. Clearly, the factors which are significant in this area, are subtle and complex. Talking about adoption may either indicate that adoptive parents are uneasy about this subject and wish to make it clear that the child does not fully 'belong' to their family, or that they are relaxed and do not feel that social and emotional bonds are any less valid than biological ties. Extremes in either direction would suggest ambivalent or distorted relationships which would not bode well for satisfactory outcome.

In addition to straightforward follow-up studies, some researchers have compared adopted children with their non-adopted peers in order to assess whether the former group's social, emotional, or educational adjustment reflect commonly occurring problems which may be related to their adoptive status. A generally optimistic picture emerges with few noteworthy exceptions. Hoopes *et al.* did not find a greater degree of maladjustment or psychopathology among 100 adopted children when their responses to objective and projective personality tests were compared with those of a matched non-adopted group. Working with adopted children as part of the National Child Development Study, Seglow *et al.* remark that, 'comparisons between the adopted and all the other children in the cohort showed few overall differences in their behaviour and adjustment in school at the age of seven years (Seglow *et al.*, 1972, p. 144). Witmer *et al.* noted no variation between adopted and non-adopted children in IQ or school achievement but did detect some small, but statistically significant differences, in favour of the latter group on a number of adjustment measures. When allowance was made for those adopted children who had been placed at over one month old, only one difference between the two groups remained statistically significant and this was a *slight* indication that adopted children were more aggressive than their non-adopted peers. Elonen and Schwartz payed particular attention to those potential difficulties which might be expected to characterise adoption, such as low self-esteem and identity confusion in attempting to integrate two sets of parents. However, such problems did not appear to be significant to adopted children and the authors conclude that, 'in essence this investigation indicates that adopted children do not have additional emotional and social problems just because they are adopted . . . as with all children, adopted or non-adopted, problems stem from their parents' reactions to them, to their questions and feelings and to important events in family life' (Elonen and Schwartz, 1969, p. 78).

Several studies have identified the particular vulnerability of adopted boys in relation to adjustment problems at home and in school. Seglow *et al.*, found, for example, that adopted children being reared in middle-class homes showed a higher level of maladjustment than other cohort children living in similar environments. A comparison of adopted and other cohort girls in middle-class homes did not confirm any difference in adjustment. It would appear, in this case, that social class was the most significant variable closely followed by gender.

Lambert and Streather's research on children from the National Child Development study showed that, at eleven years old, the adopted group had failed to maintain the favourable position in relation to other cohort children which had been measured by Seglow *et al.* four years previously. Adopted children, and particularly boys, had not progressed as well as legitimate children in the cohort during the intervening years. Attempting to make sense of this data Lambert and Streather make several observations. First, they suggest that by the age of eleven few, if any, of the adopted children would have been ignorant of their adoptive status and many of them would have started to come to terms with the fact that they had two sets of parents and the implications of this for their sense of identity. In commenting on her own research Farber (1977) suggests that relatively young children show little interest in their adoptive status because their concrete and egocentric thinking and lack of cognitive skills prohibits a full awareness of what adoption means. For the idea of adoption to have any significance, children must be able to understand that their parents did not give birth to them, and that further, another set of unknown parents did give birth to them and relinquished them to an adoptive family. Farber postulates that these propositions could not be cognitively handled by children at an early age. Secondly, by the age of eleven the task of understanding and integrating the idea of adoption would be complicated by approaching puberty. Thirdly, any strains or conflict within adoptive families may have been brought to the attention of teachers with the possibility that they reported the behaviour of children in this group in a different way to that of other children. Fourthly, other researchers (for example, Bohman, 1971 and Raynor, 1980) have pointed to the likelihood that adopted children may have some problems in middle childhood which are resolved as they get older, and this suggestion is reinforced by Clarke (1981) on the basis of her review of research studies. Information from follow-up studies of adult adoptees also supports this view, as will be appreciated from the foregoing discussion which identified satisfactory outcome in around 75 per cent or more of cases.

Some observations

Summing up his own attempts to unravel the complex factors which may influence adoption outcome Fanshel says, 'I emerge from the research experience very much aware that the task of predicting the outcome of a human experience such as adoption involves many elusive and unmeasurable elements at this stage of our research competence' (Fanshel, 1972, p. 327). This is undoubtedly so but, as he goes on to say, research may sensitise social workers to some important aspects of adoption practice and can certainly dispel some firmly held, but unsubstantiated beliefs.

The foregoing discussion suggests that to eschew adoption for children who cannot grow up with their parents because 'it doesn't work' is simply not a tenable position. Follow-up studies concluded by the time adoptees reach adolescence and young adulthood show that satisfactory outcome is achieved in the great majority of cases. Moreover, even where children have joined their new families following a period of stress or disruption, it would appear that appropriate placement can do much to ameliorate the effects of such potentially damaging experiences. It seems unlikely that most families, adoptive or not, would not point to some strain or conflict during the course of their children growing up. Kellmer-Pringle questions the emphasis on measuring 'success' in adoptions. She asserts that 'this question is rarely asked about biological parents nor, indeed, do generally acceptable criteria exist according to which judgements could be made . . . similarly the prevalence of emotional maladjustment among children of various ages and stages of development is not known' (Kellmer-Pringle, 1967, p. 26).

It is also important to note that follow-up studies have *not* identified any invariably occurring difficulties for adoptive parents or their children which arise from the social, rather than biological basis of adoption arrangements. The most significant factors in adoption outcome seem to relate to qualitative, and not easily measured, attributes of individuals and the way in which these interact to enable confident, flexible, concerned and warm parenting. In such families adopted children are able to feel secure, unconditionally loved and wanted, comfortable with the knowledge of their adoptive status and free to explore the past in a way which does not threaten relationships with their parents or the integral place which they hold in their adoptive families. There is no indication that adoption is *automatically* problematic for parents or children because of its essentially social nature.

What's the problem?

Despite the reassuring findings of many follow-up studies, professional ambivalence about adoption seems to persist beyond an appreciation of knowledge which we have gained in this way. It is likely, therefore, that there are other factors at work which relate to the 'man-made' nature of adoptive families, the motivation of prospective adopters, the psychological well-being of adopted children, and a perceived artificiality in adoption arrangements.

When assessing what makes for rewarding relationships, most of us would stress the quality and continuity of social interaction, shared experiences, joint activities, commonly held values, and so on. That is, the social nature of human activity as a basis for shared understanding, communication, and mutually understood ways of behaving towards each other within a culturally prescribed framework of expectations. When it comes to parents and their children, however, we find the situation complicated by feelings about parental rights and the recognition that biological relatedness precedes social relationships. As many commentators have pointed out, the language which we use to describe parental status assumes and denotes a hierarchy of values. Biological parents are commonly referred to as 'real' or 'natural' parents. Krugman (1964) noted, for example, that Schechter (1960) used the word 'real' seventeen times and term 'own' twice when referring to biological parents of adopted children, while neither term was used to identify adoptive parents. This terminology is frequently found in social work literature on adoption, and as Krugman suggests appears 'to grow out of a primary acceptance of a biologically oriented definition of the reality of parenthood'. Following from this, 'the converse, that the adoptive parents must then be not real, or less real becomes implicit' (Krugman, 1964, p. 353).

In terms of practice, Kellmer-Pringle asserts that 'we so over-value the child's ties with his natural parents that we are far too slow to consider severing them permanently, when the parents are disturbed or rejecting even to a pathological degree' (Kellmer-Pringle, 1975, p. 156).

Adoptive parents: a problem?

It has been suggested that an inability to conceive may be causally related to certain psychological factors which may later influence the adoptive parent–child relationship. Such psychodynamic factors are, moreover, assumed to operate not only in those cases where investigations reveal no pathology or dysfunction, but also where organic pathology is demonstrated during infertility investigations. In other words, psychodynamic disturbance may be understood to underlie and causally influence the development of organic pathology, presenting the condition described by Sandler (1961) as a 'drive to remain sterile'. The basis of this aversion to parenthood has been variously interpreted as an unconscious denial of sexuality, a defence of disturbed personalities against pregnancy and motherhood, fear of pregnancy and childbirth, anxiety, insecurity or guilt about capacity for parenthood, immature personality, faulty learning about sexual roles, disturbed relationships with own parents (more particularly mothers) and lack of perceived permission to become pregnant. Given the number of involuntarily childless couples who apply to adopt both babies and older children, psychodynamic factors associated with infertility would arguably be influential in the development of parent–child relationships and would differentiate adoptive relationships from those between biologically related parents and children who presumably would remain untouched by the 'drive to remain sterile' and its psychological determinants.

Clinical studies have attempted to clarify this area by comparing the psychological adjustment of infertile couples with that of couples who had conceived without apparent difficulty. Mai *et al.*'s (1972a) hypothesis that 'infertile wives are more likely to exhibit psychiatric pathology than fertile wives' was *not* supported by their findings. However, infertile wives were rated as being more hysterical and aggressive than others and it is suggested that these characteristics may be related to problems of sexual adjustment. Extending this research, Mai *et al.* divided their sample into three groups comprising those cases where a clearly diagnosed anatomical condition accounted for lack of conception, those where the cause of infertility was physiological, and those where no organic explanation could be found and psychological factors might therefore be assumed to be operating. No differences between the three groups were identified on any of the psychiatric measures, a result which led the authors to conclude that 'the absence of an anatomical or physiological cause for infertility per se is not sufficient for assuming the presence of psychogenic factors' (Mai *et al.*, 1972b). Further research by Platt *et al.* (1973) noted that infertile men and women saw the source of control over their lives as being external to themselves, viewed their present selves as being less similar to their ideal selves and their concepts of parents, than did fertile couples. Infertile women were assessed as being more anxious, more neurotic, less able to make decisions, than women in the fertile group.

Seward *et al.* (1965) approached their research with the assumption that 'underlying the conscious wish for a child indicated by the couple's seeking medical help was a deeper, unconscious wish to avoid reproduction'. However, comparative tests indicated that 'the similarities between the infertile women in this study and their controls were greater than the differences'. Other clinical researchers have reviewed the literature on this subject and it is clear that no firm conclusions can be drawn from available data. There is *no* evidence to demonstrate that any differences between fertile and infertile individuals are related to the cause rather than outcome of lack of conception.

Another approach to this problem is reflected by the large number of studies which have attempted to assess the folklore surrounding adoption as a 'cure' for infertility. What has not been demonstrated either theoretically or empirically is how and why adoption may relieve psychodynamic blocks to conception and as Mai (1971) points out, even those authors providing detailed case studies have not shown how this mechanism is supposed to work. Without adequate explanation, it seems equally likely that adoption would reinforce the significance of such factors rather than removing them. A large number of empirical studies have set out to measure the impact of adoption on infertility, by following up infertile patients who have subsequently adopted and comparing their conception rate with that of couples who have chosen not to adopt. Detailed references to these studies are provided in the Guide to Further Reading, but, in summary, available data do *not* support the existence of any causal relationship between adoption and subsequent conception, no matter how intuitively attractive such as association might appear.

Of course, it is possible that in *some* circumstances adoption may influence conception, but we do not, as yet, understand this process and should not assume the significance of invariably operating psychodynamic factors. Since this is the case, there is no good reason unless we are otherwise alerted, to suppose that infertile adoption applicants will commonly suffer long-standing personality problems which set them apart from others. They will undoubtedly be disappointed, frustrated and probably angry. Some responses may show a marked similarity to grief reactions found in other situations of loss. This is hardly surprising, given the unpleasant and uncertain nature of infertility investigations, management problems relating to expectations of self and others, and a readjustment process which, for many couples, means reassessing a taken-for-granted future and relinquishing plans for parenthood. It is the social and emotional aspects of this process which are likely to be of interest to social workers in adoption, rather than the significance of mysterious psychodynamic factors which, thus far, remains empirically un-demonstrated and open to question.

Adopted children: a problem?

The most significant stumbling block for many social workers seems to concern the essentially social nature of adoptive relationships and the separation of adopted children from their biological lineage. This perceived problem becomes even more important when older children are placed for adoption and thus apparently lose touch with their backgrounds and significant others. It is suggested that adopted children have no satisfactory 'roots', that their sense of identity may be impaired, that fantasies develop to compensate for the loss of biological parents, that children suffer a sense of 'genealogical bewilderment' and so on.

Freud's (1957) notion of the 'family romance' suggests that at a particular developmental stage children may fantasise about imaginary parents, usually superior in social rank and having all the desirable attributes which are considered to be lacking in their own parents. The family romance theme is asserted to pose particular problems for adopted children because their fantasy about an alternative set of parents is aligned with reality. In this case adopted children are more readily able to split a total image of their parents as being good and bad, permissive and restrictive, giving and withhold-ing, and to attribute good characteristics to one set of parents and bad characteristics to another. Authors writing from clinical experience have applied interpretations arising from the family romance to understanding apparent identity problems in adoptees (see, for example, Eiduson and Livermore, 1952; Simon and Senturia, 1966; Wieder, 1977). Following this line of investigation Schechter asserted, 'it would appear that children who have been adopted have potentially a more fertile soil for development of neurotic and psychotic states' (Schechter, 1960, p. 55). In order to assess properly the likelihood of identity-related problems in adoptees it is necessary to consider non-clinical samples. Unfortunately, research has tended to concentrate on those adoptees with adjustment difficulties but some evidence is available from other sources.

Data from Schwartz' (1970) study indicate that there were no significant differences between adopted and non-adopted boys with respect to their perceived status in the family or their perception of adoptive parents as role models. Feelings of parental rejection were no more common among the adopted children and ambivalent attitudes towards parents were expressed by all children to a similar degree. Problems of superego formation were not found among the adopted boys and Schwartz notes that children in this group showed 'adequate expression of impulse controls and acceptance of the basic values and prohibitions of their parents'. The greatest difference between the two groups emerged from responses to the Children's Thematic Apperception Tests; twenty-three of the adopted children suggested at least one adoption-related theme, but in only two cases were the biological parents perceived as being particularly 'good' in comparison with adoptive parents. In general, when reference was made to biological parents, this was in terms of curiosity regarding physical appearance, and in a third of cases children extended their interest to ask why they had been placed for adoption. However, the adopted children did not create fantasised alternative parents, their interest in biological parents was limited, and there was no evidence of difficulty in identifying with adoptive parents, identity confusion, or faulty superego formation.

Farber's (1977) comparative study confirms Schwartz' general findings, and research carried out in Denmark by Eldret *et al*. (1976) on a sample of 216 adopted adults reaches similar conclusions. Krugman (1964), from her appraisal of over fifty adopted children aged between three and seven years, found very little evidence of fantasies regarding biological parents or any splitting of identity between those perceived as 'good' and 'bad' parents. From the limited evidence available there is no reason to suppose that, in general, the actuality of having two sets of parents is necessarily of any significance to adopted children. It may well be the case that if adoptive parents are rejecting or ambivalent towards their child, or present a rejecting and negative picture of biological parents, difficulties are likely to arise in connection with family romance themes, identity, and the development of self-esteem. However, these problems are *not* a necessary and invariable consequence of adoption.

It has also been suggested that telling children about their adoptive status before they have resolved anxieties around the Oedipus complex, may lead to difficulties in completing this resolution successfully. It may also prompt fears about separation and abandonment, incestuous threat, castration anxiety and 'not belonging' (see, for example, Peller, 1961). If adopted children show no significant reaction to information about their adoptive status, there seems to be an assumption of 'deeper, non-observable feelings and reactions to the event' (Schechter, 1964, p. 1114). The alleged importance of timing communication about adoption in relation to the Oedipal phase is simply *not* supported by empirical evidence from non-clinical studies or from follow-up assessments of adoption outcome. As has previously been noted, the significance of telling depends largely on the quality of parent–child relationships and overall family functioning rather than on specific and invariant factors which are 'built into' adoption.

Problems are also assumed to arise from a discontinuity of biological ancestry. Writing about the problems of nineteen teenage adoptees, Frisk (1964) suggests that because they have been separated from their biological parents, they have no known 'genetic ego.' Social identity developed in an adoptive family becomes insufficient for self-recognition once adolescence is reached, and a new identity must be found which integrates genetic factors, thus laying the 'hereditary ghost' of biological antecedents. Sants (1977) defines the genealogically bewildered child as one who has no, or only uncertain, knowledge about his biological parents. He argues that this lack of knowledge is significant for several reasons. First, as the child begins to mature he will come to feel attached to the whole family of which he is part, including ancestors and those alive at the present. The genealogically deprived child is apparently hampered by 'not knowing which clan or family he belongs to'. Secondly, Sants argues that differences in physical appearance and lack of a genetic relationship can severely hinder a child's ability to identify with adoptive parents. Thirdly, and deriving from Freud's suggestion that there is a 'universal deep seated fear of incest', Sants asserts that insufficient knowledge about origins may lead to fear of unknowingly committing incest. It would appear then that no adopted child could escape a sense of genealogical bewilderment, no matter how well informed and able the adoptive parents might be. However, it must be pointed out once again that the importance placed on biological continuity by Sants and others is *not* confirmed by empirical evidence.

Adopted children and child psychiatric services

Attention has been focused on whether adopted children are referred for psychiatric help more frequently than children growing up with their biological parents. This question presents complex issues of measurement and comparison and I doubt that we have, as yet, reached a satisfactory answer. Schechter was one of the first clinical researchers to make some alarming comments about this matter. In 1960 he reported that of 125 children seen in his private practice from 1948 to 1953, sixteen or 13.3 per cent had been adopted compared with 0.134 per cent of adopted children in the general population of the United States. He states that 'this indicates a hundred-fold increase of patients in this category as seen in my practice, compared with what could be expected in the general population'.

Further research carried out in the United States by Sweeny *et al.* (1963), Borgatta and Fanshel (1965), Kirk *et al.* (1966), Simon and Senturia (1966) and Toussieng (1962) indicates that adopted children referred to child guidance and psychiatric services outnumber the proportion which would normally be expected. Goodman *et al.* (1963), however, arrived at a different conclusion. They analysed the closed cases of children seen at the Staten Island Mental Health Centre during the seven-year period of 1956–62. This involved 593 children of whom fourteen or 2.4 per cent had been adopted by non-relatives. The authors were careful to compare the number in the *local* community, rather than with the estimated number in the general population. On the basis of this analysis they conclude that 'the rate of extra-familial, locally adopted children being brought to a child psychiatric clinic within the community of their adoption may be lower than that for biological children'. In Britain research on this topic has been more limited, although work by Kellmer-Pringle (1961) and Humphrey and Ounstead (1963) does suggest that adopted children referred for psychiatric advice were disproportionately represented at the time of their studies. However, the NAMH survey (1953) of 1,152 adopted children did not find this to be the case.

Researchers have not only been interested in the number of children referred for psychiatric help, but in attempting to differentiate between the symptomatology of adopted and non-adopted children. If children experience developmental difficulties because of some factors which are *essentially* related to their adoptive status, then one might expect to identify specific symptoms which are amenable to consistent theoretical explanation. Menlove compared fifty-one adopted and non-adopted children referred for psychiatric assessment, on nine aggressive type symptoms, four aggressive type syndromes and a range of non-aggressive type symptoms. The two groups of children were only found to be significantly different in relation to hyperactivity, hostility and negativism, these three symptoms being more pronounced in the adopted children.

Several authors have noted that adopted children tend to be diagnosed as having more 'aggressive type' symptoms than non-adopted children. These have been variously described as defiance towards parents, unwillingness to assume responsibility, problems of task orientation, anti-social and aggressive behaviour towards peers (see, for example, Humphrey and Ounstead, 1963; Reece and Levin,

1968; Offord *et al.*, 1969; Work and Anderson, 1971). In two studies
these findings have been contradicted. Raleigh (1954) discovered 'few
noteworthy differences' between adopted and non-adopted boys,
attending the Institute for Juvenile Research in Chicago, for emotional disturbance. The former group tended to be less severely
disturbed and it was the latter group which showed greater aggres-
siveness in school and social relationships. Sweeny *et al.* (1963)
concluded from their comparative research that adopted and non-
adopted children did not differ significantly in terms of symptoms or
diagnoses.

At first glance, the apparently high proportion of adopted children
referred for psychiatric help appears to be dramatic. We must ask,
however, whether the authors of these studies have adequately
estimated the proportion of adopted children in the general population and whether such an estimate constitutes an appropriate
baseline for comparison. If a relatively high referral rate is demonstrated, does this then mean that there is something intrinsic to
adoption which makes adopted children, in general, more prone to
emotional maladjustment than their non-adopted peers? In relation
to the first question, Schechter has been severely criticised for his
method of estimating the proportion of adopted children in the
general population. He determined the ratio between the number of
children for whom adoption petitions were filed during 1953 and the
child population in 1953. His estimate would have been considerably
modified if he had more appropriately compared all adopted children
in the population with the total child population of 1953.

Some writers have taken account of social class distribution in
different areas, suggesting that predominantly middle-class popula-
tions would be likely to have a higher proportion of adopted children
and possibly be more likely to seek professional advice. They would
therefore recommend that the proportion of adopted children should
be calculated for a local rather than the general population. Kadushin
(1966) suggests that it is invalid to make general comparisons
between the proportion of adopted children referred for psychiatric
advice and others, without also considering the operation of similar
risk factors in family structure and interaction. Thus, he argues, the
appropriate comparison group of non-adopted children would comprise those 'living in middle-class families who were born to older
non-adoptive parents as their first child and who are the only children
in such families'. Although this picture has undoubtedly changed
since Kadushin was writing, his reminder that researchers should
compare 'like the like' is an important point. The Children's Bureau
in the United States estimated that approximately 1 per cent of the

total child and youth population are adopted by non-relatives and a further 1 per cent by relatives. However, these findings were subsequently re-examined by Jonassohn (1965) who concluded that the prevalence of adopted children in the under twenty-one age group would be closer to 3 per cent for all adoptions or 1.5 per cent for non-relative adoptions. Any association between adoption and the prevalence of psychiatric referral rates remains problematic and open to argument.

Conclusion

It is important, when considering adoption, not only to grasp what knowledge we have available but to be aware of those areas which are still open to exploration and debate and where caution must be employed in making judgements. When social workers are responsible for rational planning and decision-making and intent upon demonstrating professional skills, it is difficult to accept that an antipathy towards adoption may stem from the feeling that it is somehow unnatural, that the 'blood tie' makes for some mysterious bond, or that social interaction cannot adequately replace biology as a basis for successful parenting. We must be clear about those aspects of practice which are relevant and which may be improved, and those beliefs about adoption which may be deeply held but mistakenly based.

Several points should be noted about the research which has been discussed in this chapter. First, follow-up studies demonstrate that adoption can work well for a whole range of children and factors which may influence outcome are not intrinsically related to the adoption experience. Secondly, there is no evidence that couples who fail to conceive suffer from any distinguishing psychological problems which will necessarily affect their capacity for successful adoptive parenthood. There are likely to be contingent difficulties which relate to the unpleasant and uncertain nature of infertility investigations, re-definition of marriage and goals, loss of control and ability to plan, and social management of childlessness. It is probably the outcome of couples' attempts to grapple with these areas that will influence their parenting ability rather than any invariably occurring psychodynamic factors. Thirdly, it has been suggested that the biological discontinuity which characterises adoption arrangements will cause adoptees to suffer from 'genealogical bewilderment' with associated problems of identity confusion, insecurity and poor self-image. Interpreting the significance of these problems also concerns the emphasis which we place on biological relatedness for valid and successful parent–child relationships, and our values about who are a child's 'real' parents. The development of identity and self-esteem is a complex business taking place in the context of interaction with significant others and influenced by a variety of individual and social factors. Difficulties may arise in a number of areas including ambivalent or hostile family relationships, distorted or limited communication, inconsistent parental responses, and for adopted children particularly, anxiety or lack of information about their background and reasons for placement. The important question, however, is whether adoption *necessarily* causes identity problems for children who are separated from their biological parents. Non-clinical and follow-up studies suggest that this is *not* the case.

Fourthly, we must recognise those areas in which difficulties may arise for adopted children. Clinical studies have based their conclusions on information about a selected group of children referred to child psychiatric services, rather than on an assessment of the actual frequency of emotional problems among adopted, as compared to non-adopted children. Where problems are indicated, for example in the case of boys adopted as only children into middle-class families or in relation to age of children on placement, a combination of several factors seems likely to influence outcome. Similarly, adjustment problems of adopted children at around eleven years old, which may be expressed particularly in school, do not appear to be longstanding or essentially related to some invariant characteristics of adoptive relationships. It was further reported at a meeting of the American Psychiatric Association in 1969, that random sample comparisons of adopted and non-adopted children did not provide any evidence that the former group suffered a higher incidence of emotional maladjustment or psychopathology than the latter (Child Adoption, 1970, No. 2). Clearly the information at our disposal does not warrant categorical or simplistic assertions that adopted children are generally more vulnerable to emotional difficulties because adoptive relationships are *inherently* stressful or problematic.

Fifthly, follow-up studies can only assess the outcome of adoptions which were arranged many years ago. Over time there has been a significant change in social attitudes towards illegitimacy, an increasing awareness of the part played by environmental and social factors in human development, a growing openness in recognising and accepting the adoptive status of parents and children, and widening choices relating to lifestyles and parenting. Adoption now has a public face and is brought to our attention by such organisations as British Agencies for Adoption and Fostering and Parent to Parent

Information on Adoption Services. Involuntary childlessness is also something which can now be discussed, whatever the personal pain, and groups such as 'The National Association for the Childless' in Britain and 'Resolve' in the United States have done much to ensure that this subject has been brought to public attention. All these factors are likely to facilitate more, rather than less, satisfactory outcomes to adoption placements. Clearly any decision to place a child for adoption must be based on available knowledge and a careful analysis of each situation. However, what we already know about this subject indicates that we may choose adoption with a high degree of confidence that this will work well for adopted children and their new families.

3

Making Plans and Choosing Resources

It seemed to me, even, that there was nothing more fragile on all the
Earth. In the moonlight I looked at his pale forehead, his closed eyes, his
locks of hair that trembled in the wind, and I said to myself: what I see
here is nothing but a shell. What is most important is invisible.

Antoine de Saint-Exupery, *The Little Prince*

Introduction

Social work in adoption will involve decision-making from the word
go. There will be policy decisions about the work to be covered,
immediate 'rationing' of applicants by area, age, religion and possibly
other characteristics, the procedure for assessing/preparing applicants, the composition and function of the adoption panel, sharing of
information with prospective adopters, intensity and duration of
introductions, placement, post placement and possibly post adoption
support, the payment of adoption allowances (Section 32, Children
Act 1975). Throughout the procedure, social workers will be making
decisions about prospective adopters' understanding of, and ability to
cope with, the tasks of adoptive parenthood, the kind of child they
could realistically and successfully parent, readiness for introductions, reactions to particular children, degree of attachment and
commitment, the appropriate time for placement, and later adoption.

However, as has been indicated earlier, decisions must be made
where parents have asked for adoption, and also where children are in
care but parents refuse to agree to a permanent placement with
prospective adopters. Such decisions must take into account parents'
rights, the child's welfare, the parents' willingness and ability to work
towards rehabilitation, time limits which may be imposed on
rehabilitation plans given the child's age, previous experience and
other factors, the child's need for secure and permanent relationships and willingness to accept these. Not a bad list! In order to make
appropriate decisions we must have relevant knowledge. We have

already considered what is known about the nature of adoptive relationships and outcome. From this it is possible to assess how social workers may improve practice to enhance the quality of adoption placements and to safeguard a child's future with his adoptive family. It also suggests that adoption is a realistic choice for many children who cannot grow up with their biological parents. An essential part of decision-making in adoption must relate to children's needs and those circumstances in which adoption would be considered to be in a child's best interest.

A great deal has been written about the needs and rights of children, some of it empirically derived, and some of it based on the feelings, values and ideological inclinations of the writers concerned. The factors which influence individual development are complex and as we all know some children will come through appalling experiences relatively unscathed while others may succumb to the impact of minor disruptions and conflicts. However, such complexity does not relieve either parents or social workers of the responsibility to ensure that children grow up in the kind of environment which is likely to provide opportunities for developing confidence, self-esteem, communication and interaction skills, trust, the capacity for forming relationships, social controls, and knowledge. In other words, the elements of affective and cognitive functioning which enable us to understand the world in which we live and to engage in appropriate social interaction with other people who share it.

The needs of children

What then can we reasonably say about the needs of children? Kellmer-Pringle (1975) has taken a look at available research and concludes that there are four basic emotional needs which must be met if children are going to grow up into capable and confident adults. First, she suggests the need for love and security, probably the most important in terms of forming the basis for an ability to make rewarding relationships with an ever widening circle of people. Many researchers and writers have commented on the difficulty of defining and measuring the qualitative aspects of love. However, it seems likely that we would understand it to comprise a concern to enhance another's well-being through providing rewarding exchanges and experiences, physical affection, and providing for life-maintaining needs such as warmth, food, sleep and protection from danger. A sense of security is provided by continuous and reliable relationships with significant others, while predictability and familiar routine enable children to feel safe as they encounter new experiences and changing situations.

Secondly, children have a need to explore and to be stimulated by increasing information and novel experiences, in order to develop intelligence, confidence and a sense of control over the world in which they live. The most important elements here are opportunities for social interaction, play, and the mastery of language. Play facilitates learning about the world, working out solutions and using fantasy to broaden experience and understanding. Kellmer-Pringle asserts that probably the most crucial factor for intellectual ability is the quality of the 'language environment'. That is, not only the amount of conversation, but the range and 'richness' of language used and the content and breadth of linguistic exchanges. Clearly, language development depends also on the process of social interaction, first as the basis for actually learning a vocabulary and rules for linking words, and secondly as the way in which children come to understand the meaning of social exchanges, interpreting what is said to them and responding appropriately.

The third need of children identified by Kellmer-Pringle is for praise and recognition. As she points out, growing up into a socially able adult requires a vast amount of emotional, social and intellectual learning which must be sustained and developed throughout the years. Until children are old enough to appreciate the inherent satisfaction of a 'job well done' there must be some incentive to help them through the frustration, conflict, disappointment and sometimes confusion of learning how to be socially and intellectually competent. Recognition, encouragement and praise from significant others provide such incentives. It is also important to note that expectations and responses should depend on knowledge and awareness of an individual child's capabilities. Inappropriate demands, which deny the possibility of achievement and praise, may lead to frustration, anger or withdrawal. Fourthly, children need to develop a sense of responsibility through personal independence. In order to express this in a socially acceptable way, limits and controls must first be established for young children by their significant others. It is within this framework that increasing leeway may gradually be given to children to choose between options, to decide on plans and actions, to make their own friends, to feel responsible for others, to accept the consequences of choices, and so on.

Although Kellmer-Pringle has identified what she believes to be generally relevant needs, she makes the important point that meeting these needs must be geared to the characteristics, personalities and capabilities of individual children. Recognising and responding appropriately to these factors depends on continuity of social interaction and developing knowledge of particular children. For this reason, Kellmer-Pringle argues that children's needs cannot be adequately met in residential care, or in situations where relationships between children and their parents or other caretakers are continually interrupted by separation or changes in caretaking figures.

Rutter (1981) has provided a thorough overview and analysis of available research. He is very careful to make it clear that the whole process of child development is complex, and that questions about the significance of bonding and its relation to attachment and separation are still unresolved. However, he suggests on the basis of cumulative research we may now take for granted that 'many infants show developmental retardation following admission to a poor quality institution and may exhibit intellectual impairment if they remain there for a long time; that there is an association between delinquency and broken homes; that affectionless psychopathy sometimes follows multiple separation experiences and institutional care in early childhood; and that dwarfism is particularly seen in children from rejecting and affectionless homes'. Different aspects of early developmental experiences have a differential impact on the specific nature of problems at a later stage.

Several points may be extracted from Rutter's detailed discussion. First, undue emphasis has been placed on the mother–child relationship – the crucial factor is the quality of the relationship itself and other people may have more significance in this respect. Secondly, experience of multiple caretakers is not necessarily problematic provided the standard of care is good and caretaking individuals remain the same. Thirdly, separation, as such, is not usually the critical variable in causing distress or developmental problems. Difficulties may arise from multiple separations, particularly when combined with other negative factors, and the quality of relationships prior to separation will affect reactions to it. Fourthly, anti-social disorders arising from the divorce of parents and broken homes are associated not with separation, but with discord and disharmony in family relationships which preceded the disruption. Affectionless psychopathy is due, not to breaking of relationships, but to an initial failure to form bonds and develop attachments. Similarly intellectual impairment is related to a lack of appropriate stimulation, rather than the experience of separation only. Thus Rutter stresses the development, maintenance and quality of relationships and interaction as being significant in influencing development. Lack of attachment or distorted relationships do not bode well for a child's future. Fifthly,

Rutter examines the notion of critical phases of development and concludes that evidence to support this is not forthcoming. Apart from early lack of attachment, difficulties may arise throughout childhood and be ameliorated by a return to an environment in which the damaging factors are no longer present. Sixthly, is the finding that *single* isolated chronic stresses may not cause later disorders. However, a combination of two or more chronic stresses appears to have an interactive rather than merely an additive effect. Rutter also notes the importance of transactional effects where one stress actually increases the likely occurrence of others, for example, more frequent admissions to hospital in children from deprived families.

It would appear then, from Rutter's critical overview of research, that a lack of opportunity to develop attachments and the presence of distorted or discordant relationships are significant factors in problematic development. Although separation must be distinguished from bond disruption, the return of children to such environments of chronic stress or multiple stresses is likely to have a profoundly negative influence on subsequent development.

What happens to children in care?

Summing up the feelings of ten individuals who had experienced long-term care during the period 1942–69, Kahan says that 'there was too little continuity, too much fragmentation, they had a sense of damaged identity, feelings of helplessness and isolation in the face of events and people taking charge of them, they felt they lost their childhood before they had lived through it' (Kahan, 1979, p. 184). While well-meaning people were beavering away on behalf of these children, they felt alone, confused, frightened and unable to control what was happening to them. I have already referred to the sobering findings of Rowe and Lambert (1973). Crucially, their study demonstrated that, at the time, there were still large numbers of children being brought up in care, and there is no evidence to suggest that this picture has significantly changed. Sixty-one per cent of the 2,812 children studied were expected to remain in care until they reached eighteen. Very few children (5 per cent) saw both their parents as often as once a month, 18 per cent saw one parent at least once a month and 35 per cent saw one or both parents occasionally. There was no parental contact for 41 per cent of children. Rowe and Lambert point out that the longer children remain in care the less likely they are to have contact with parents, a finding also confirmed in Lasson's study of seventy-two children in care, and one which common sense could reasonably predict.

Adcock (1981) suggests that key factors which are likely to be harmful for children who have come into care from deprived and already damaging family situations, are changes in placement, instability and rejection by caretakers, the child's sense of insecurity and impermanence of present placements. Children in care may go on to suffer the same kinds of experiences' with the possibility of an interactive effect as described by Rutter. This may involve foster home breakdown, and Adcock refers to a number of studies showing that the longer children remain in care the more likely they are to have experienced an increasing number of moves (see Rowe and Lambert, 1973; Fanshel and Shinn, 1978; and research documented in Prosser, 1978).

In Martin's (1976) study of fifty-eight abused children it was found that twenty of the children had been subjected to between three and eight changes of home in four and a half years. He makes the oft-quoted and somewhat emotive remark that 'like the lemmings in their fatalistic march to the sea we find child abuse teams sentencing children to new traumas which may cause more emotional scars and havoc than the abusive environment from which they came'. Thus Adcock suggests that being in care may subject children to further emotional deprivation and disruption, and that if they cannot return home in the short term, permanent alternative placements should be sought for them. However, she also argues that residential and foster care cannot provide the security of permanence and that this may only be achieved through adoption.

One of the major reasons for eschewing adoption of children in care concerns the importance of continued contact between children and their parents. Legal, professional and parental concern about this area has recently found a response in those matters relating to access in The Health and Social Services and Social Security (Adjudications) Act, 1983. The debate has several facets. It is argued that placement for adoption, and termination of access without parental agreement, disregards the rights of parents to see their children and to maintain the possibility of having them home. The Working Party on Fostering Practice (1976) recommends encouraging parental contact on the grounds that it provides children with a link to their past, is necessary for the appropriate development of identity, and faces children with reality rather than allowing the growth of fantasies which idealise parents and blame social workers or foster parents for a failure to return home. Holman (1975) cites several research studies in support of his argument for an 'inclusive' fostering model.

Weinstein (1960) found that *regular* parental contact was associated with higher scores for foster children on present and future 'well-being' scales. Jenkins (1969) asserts that 57 per cent of foster children whom she studied and who were over 1½ years old on placement, were 'disturbed' where there was no parental contact, compared to only 35 per cent of those with regular contact. Thorpe's (1974) well-known research established an association between foster children's adjustment and their understanding of fostering and the role of the Children's Department. Children who were in contact with their parents had a significantly better understanding of family background, reasons for being in care and the part played by the Children's Department and social workers. The relationship between satisfactory adjustment and parental contact was only statistically significant for eleven to thirteen year olds. Holman (1973) also observed from his own research findings that, generally, less parental contact was associated with a higher incidence of certain physical and emotional problems.

Holman also suggests that 'inclusive' fostering which is open to regular parental contact, and where foster parents are quite clear about their role as caretakers on behalf of others, is likely to facilitate successful outcome. He argues that an 'exclusive' model encourages foster parents to perceive themselves as more like biological or adoptive parents. This situation may well deprive foster children of information about their backgrounds, and create role conflict and confusion for foster parents whose anxiety may permeate family relationships. It is certainly the case that research on the perceptions of long-term foster parents has indicated a high proportion operating an 'exclusive' model with consequent confusion about their role *vis-à-vis* foster children, social workers, and biological parents.

In essence, therefore, long-term fostering may be preferred to adoption for children in care because parental contact may be maintained. This arrangement, it is suggested, affirms the rights of parents, is conducive to the welfare of children, and when related to an 'inclusive' model of fostering, is more likely to achieve successful placements.

What are the options?

I have argued that adoption should be viewed as a realistic choice for children who cannot grow up in their own families. Making such final decisions must clearly be based on a recognition and evaluation of other options. Long-term foster home placements have been critically examined by researchers and attempts have been made to relate child and foster parent characteristics to outcome. However, as we have discovered from adoption studies, data produced in this way tend to be somewhat inconsistent, and Parker's (1966) prediction table of factors discriminating between success and failure in fostering outcome has not been validated by subsequent research (see, for example, George, 1970 and Napier, 1972). What we do know is that the 'success' rate of foster home placements, as assessed by continuity of foster parents' willingness to maintain children in their families, is relatively low. Studies have considered foster children remaining in placement for varying periods of two years to those continuing for five years. Assessment measures have relied on duration of placements rather than on the quality of family interaction or the well-being of foster children.

Whatever the differences in research design and outcome measurements used, Prosser notes that 'on both sides of the Atlantic there has been a great deal of concern expressed at the high failure rate of foster placements' and that 'a number of studies have reported success rates of around 40–50%' (Prosser, 1978, p. 13). The higher rate of satisfactory outcome which has been demonstrated for adoption does not provide an argument for automatically favouring this option. Unfortunately, research initiatives have not considered whether differences between adoption and fostering significantly influence relative outcomes, or, indeed, how such a process might work. However, information at our disposal does suggest that careful thought should be given to the most appropriate type of placement and desired plan for children who cannot grow up with their biological parents. Those social workers who emphasise planning for permanency would generally prefer adoption to the more open-ended alternative of long-term fostering.

Residential care may be viewed as another option for children unable to live with their own families, and has perhaps been subject to the greatest swings of support and criticism over the years (see, for example, Packman, 1975). Given particular circumstances, residential care may be considered the placement of choice for some children. Research and experience suggest, however, that in many cases informed choice has little to do with long-term residential placements, that once so-placed alternatives may not be actively pursued, and that children may be handicapped in terms of learning social skills, developing an acceptable self-image and sense of self-esteem, and attaining emotional maturity and stability (see Prosser, 1976). Having taken into account the factors considered above Seglow *et al.* conclude that:

the point of departure is the belief that, on the one hand, adoption is the best method of substitute care for most children whose parents are unable, unwilling or unfit to provide a suitable and permanent home for them. It is best because, if for no other reason (and there *are* other reasons) it has a far lower failure rate than residential and foster care . . . On the other hand, it is also essential to recognise that providing a permanent parental relationship for a child who needs it, is different from having children of one's own.

(Seglow *et al.*, 1972, p. 163)

Is adoption a choice?

There are clearly many reasons, elaborated in this and foregoing chapters, for social workers' ambivalence about adoption, especially for children in care. Of the twenty-eight local authorities and five voluntary agencies visited during Rowe and Lambert's study, two-thirds were busy developing fostering programmes while neglecting the possibility of adoption for at least some of the children in care. It is reported that staff in five agencies considered the rights of biological parents to be paramount and that they should never be terminated, while eight agencies had a policy of choosing long-term fostering even where children had no links with their parents.

So far we have discovered that adoption works well and that it is not *inherently* problematic for either adoptive parents or their adopted children. There is also some evidence that children in long-term care do not experience the security of permanent placements, the opportunity of developing significant and lasting relationships with consistent adults, or regular and constructive contact with their biological parents. Perhaps the most difficult area to be faced when choosing adoption relates to whether it is realistic for parents, and beneficial for children, to continue parental contact, and how far parents' rights may conflict with, and be allowed to supersede, the welfare of their children. These are emotive issues, but if social workers are to make any reasonable decisions they must be put into perspective.

The following points should be borne in mind. First, as Thorpe (1974) suggests, it may be the case that social workers are not sufficiently energetic in involving parents with decision-making about their children's future or in encouraging and facilitating continuing contact. This is reprehensible for professional workers who should be concerned with the well-being of whole families. However, we should remember that in some instances parents are so disturbed, and relationships with their children so distorted, that continuing contact may be positively damaging to children's development, identity, and sense of self-esteem. The Working Party on Fostering Practice (1976) recognises that under these circumstances parental contact should be stopped. We should also avoid making the assumption that all parents wish to maintain contact with their children. There is not a simple or essential association between biological relatedness and the existence of mutually rewarding relationships. Not long ago I was at a review where a mother was trying to explain that she did not visit her child more often because she felt no affection for him and he made her irritable and uncomfortable. This in turn made her feel angry with him and guilty about her own reactions. Unfortunately, the social workers present did not attempt to understand and accept her feelings, but conveyed the message that she really did love her child because she was his mother and her feelings were related to other problems which were making her upset. More anger and more guilt! Some parents wish to maintain contact for reasons which are unrelated to the welfare of their children. Plans to encourage and facilitate parental contact for children in long-term care must be made after careful assessment of parents' motivation and commitment, not simply because it must be good (by definition) for all parents and all children to have continued contact.

Secondly, it is possible to help children understand and retain links with their past without parental contact. Termination of contact is *not* the same as cutting children off from knowledge and understanding of their background, denying the existence of biological parents, or failing to recognise the emotional importance of past experiences and significant others. There is now a great deal of practice literature concerning working with children in order to help them understand what has happened to them and the process of compiling 'life books' which record biographical information, photographs of parents, and so on. Terminating parental contact is not meant to diminish the importance of parents but recognises the development of significant relationships with psychological parents, or 'frees' the child to establish such relationships on the basis of 'security of tenure'.

Thirdly, and bearing in mind our earlier discussion about presumed identity confusion in adopted children, it does not seem to be valid to suggest that continued parental contact is essential for the satisfactory development of a sense of identity and self-esteem. A recognition that the idea of a 'fresh start' is not appropriate for children who are joining new families and an acceptance of past experiences and individual personalities, is more important for identity and self-esteem than contact with people whose emotional and social significance has become comparatively tenuous.

Fourthly, research which indicates an association between parental contact and well-being of children in long-term foster homes must be viewed with caution. Holman (1973) actually found that while *regular* contact between parents and children was beneficial, infrequent contact was related to greater problems for children than no contact at all. Jenkins (1969) recorded similar results. Thus, as might be expected regular, predictable, and trustworthy contact would maintain parents in the role of significant others and sustain the continuity and frequency of social interaction which are necessary to avoid attenuation of relationships. If, however, parents fail to have regular contact with their children, long-term caretakers are likely to become psychological parents whether we like it or not. Broken promises, disappointments, long silences, although understandable from the parents' point of view, are likely to endanger children's sense of trust and engender feelings of rejection, badness, unacceptability and responsibility for lack of contact. Such feelings are not likely to be beneficial for the development of identity or self-esteem in children in long-term care.

Fifthly, if as research suggests, long-term foster parents tend to see themselves as akin to biological or adoptive parents then we must look again at the preparation of foster parents, their involvement in planning and decision-making, and the degree of clarity which we are able and willing to convey about the task which we are asking them to undertake. If social workers are unclear about planning for the future of children in care, then it is not surprising that foster parents become confused about their role. Not long ago I was asked to provide a foster family for a child in care. As well as information about the child I requested details about the plan, so that an appropriate placement could be allocated. It seemed that there was no intention to pursue a particular plan. The foster parents were expected to provide a short-term placement initially, which might turn into a long-term placement, which might turn into a permanent placement. It all depended! I am not suggesting that complex situations can be resolved overnight, but there appeared to be no recognition that one set of foster parents were being asked to undertake three quite different tasks with distinct role implications and requiring qualitatively specific kinds of motivation, expectations and emotional commitment. If this is the basis on which we proceed it is hardly surprising that placements suffer tension and conflicts of interest, or that foster parents (and indeed children) are confused about the nature of their relationships and the status of placements. Matching plans for children with the motivation and role expectations of foster or adoptive parents seems, to me, to be as important as matching in relation to interests, personalities, behaviour, tolerance of difficulties, family structure, and so on.

The above observations should not be understood to mean that I would dismiss lightly the needs and rights of parents or the importance of maintaining parental contact. I do not wish to polarise the arguments. I do wish to suggest, however, that neglecting the possibility of adoption because it is *assumed* that continuing parental contact is beneficial to all concerned, is not an acceptable position. In situations where there is a conflict of interest between parents and their children, I do believe that social workers have a duty to give first consideration to the need to safeguard and promote the child's welfare, if only because children are more vulnerable, have fairly well-established developmental needs, and at a relatively young age do not have the ability to make independent choices. Decisions concerning adoption must therefore depend on a critical assessment of each child's needs, the viability of rehabilitation, the degree of attachment to parents or other caretakers, significance of relationships with them and a recognition that the passage of time has different implications for children of different ages.

Good practice in child care, and particularly in adoption, requires appropriate decision-making. In making, or avoiding making decisions, social workers must not only be aware of available knowledge but must also be alert to the way in which they interpret this and the values which inform their understanding. As Shaw and Lebens have commented:

> many disputes which are on the face of it 'technical' are probably thinly disguised disagreements on questions of value concerning the rights and needs of parents and children, the sanctity or utility of the family as an institution and so on. A recent example was the way in which Weinstein's (1960) highly tentative findings on the value of parental contact for children in foster home care were elevated to the status of Holy Writ as part of the campaign against the Children Bill during 1975, suggesting a greater concern with political ideology than with research appreciation.
>
> (Shaw and Lebens, 1978, p. 20)

There is a danger that social work practice and decision-making in adoption may come to owe more to ideological debate than to an appropriate assessment of the needs of children in care.

The use and abuse of resources

I have suggested that social workers are in a poor position to criticise foster parents for feeling confused about their role and tending to operate an 'exclusive' model in long-term placements, if they are not clear about the purpose of placements at the time they are made. This means communicating certain information to foster parents, including circumstances leading to placement, the anticipated plan, any legal action which may be pending, intentions with regard to parental contact, and any factors which may require a change in the plan. If children come into care in emergencies or at very short notice, it may not be possible to provide all this information to foster parents at the time they receive a child, but it should be made available to them as soon as possible. Sometimes a placement is clearly for a short and limited period, for example when it is due to hospital admission of a mother. Other parental difficulties which involve financial or housing problems may also be resolved within a fairly short time. More complex problems relating to marital conflict, mental illness, unstable family relationships, non-accidental injury, neglect, other forms of family violence, non-school attendance, anti-social behaviour of parents and children, personality disorders in parents, and so on, may take longer to assess and involve social work intervention over a fairly long period while children remain in care.

Clearly, social workers must assess the family's circumstances and attempt to identify significant factors leading to a child's admission to care. They must then decide whether such factors are amenable to change, what kind of intervention is necessary to achieve this, and over what period such change might be accommodated, in order to allow the child to return home. In some cases social workers may make a speedy decision that it would be unacceptable for a child to be rehabilitated in the near future, if at all. This might happen if a child has experienced several previous admissions to care or where change seems unlikely, as might be the case with parents who have chronic emotional or personality problems combined with injury, neglect, or rejection of their children. The initial placement may thus be intended to be short term where there will be as much parental contact as possible and intensive work with the family to effect rehabilitation, or it may be intended, under extreme and chronic circumstances, to be long term. Whether 'long term' means for the foreseeable future, permanent, or including adoption, will depend on all the factors already discussed, but *must* take into account the child's age, and in relation to this, attachment to parents, quality of relationship with parents, ability to maintain attachment with absent parents, and the benefits of continued parental contact. Early planning may have to be modified because of changes in assessment, the appearance of additional complicating factors, inappropriate social work intervention given new or differently perceived problems, or legal action. What was intended to be a short-term placement may indeed turn out to be long term or permanent.

The important point, however, is that such a change should not occur through a process of 'drift' but should depend on assessment, planning and explicit decision-making. Throughout this process, foster parents should be sufficiently involved with developments and decisions to understand what is *intended* to be the outcome, and therefore the part which they have to play in reaching the desired goal. I recently discussed the desirability of including foster parents in statutory boarding out reviews, with a social work colleague. The social worker considered that many foster parents would not want this as they would see it as an intrusion into normal family life and it would remind them that children were still in care and the responsibility of the local authority. One up to Bob Holman! Many of the children placed with these foster parents had arrived there on a temporary basis, but had drifted into long-term placements, and finally permanent placements, without clear decisions having been made about parental contact, the pursuit of rehabilitation, desired alternatives to rehabilitation, or any acknowledgement that the nature of the placement had changed. I would suggest that at some point, social workers should have been in a position to say 'we have tried all realistic means of rehabilitation and taking all factors, including the child's age, into consideration we must now plan a secure and permanent placement for this child'. The implications of this decision would then be assessed in relation to the child's present placement and the child would either be moved to a new family, or the present caretakers would accept a clearly changed and explicitly defined role, which might or might not include adoption.

Some social workers use the kind of terminology which suggests that they have little control over outcome. Discussing a desired goal, communication may take the form of 'I hope the child will return home', 'I would like to see more parental contact', 'time will tell', 'we will have to wait and see', or 'it all depends'. All these statements may have some validity but results do not depend on hope, what we would like to see, wishes, good intentions or the passage of time. Social work intervention must *intend* certain things to happen, and presupposes active steps to achieve the intended outcome. Intentions are not hewn out of rock and may be changed on the basis of a reassessment, or nullified by the power of other decisions, for example those made by a

Court. However, unless social workers are explicit about their intentions in the first place, it is of little wonder that parents, children, and those in a day-to-day caretaking role are anxious and confused about how they relate to each other and what is likely to happen.

Clarity in the caretaking role is related to an understanding of intended outcome, but it also depends on the motivation and expectations of those who offer to care for other people's children. Some foster parents may wish to undertake short-term placements, for a number of reasons. Other people may really want to accept a child and to bring him up as a permanent member of their family. A significant proportion of this group are likely to see adoption as their primary aim. An important part of working with prospective foster or adoptive parents must be to help them consider what kind of placement they are able and willing to manage. Placements will be inappropriate and vulnerable to failure if foster parents who wish to provide temporary care find themselves in the role of long-term psychological parents, or those who want a child to stay are expected to facilitate parental contact and work towards a loss which they would prefer to avoid. Anxiety, conflict, and breakdown of place-ments are not only related to role confusion, but to inappropriate role expectations which do not take into account the needs, motivation, and aspirations of the caretakers themselves. There will clearly be some situations where short-term foster parents can accommodate a change to a long-term placement, as relationships develop and attachment grows. Some people may also be sufficiently flexible to accept a range of placements or alteration in plans. However, a failure to consider the motivation of prospective foster or adoptive parents may well lead to an abuse of family resources, loss of foster parents, and breakdown in placements.

Conclusion

An important component of social work in adoption, as indeed in all social work intervention, is making, and helping others to make, appropriate decisions. I have argued in this and previous chapters that such decisions are not always based on available knowledge, and that they are likely to be influenced by feelings, anxieties, and ideological inclinations which often, by their very nature, are not explicitly recognised. As late as 1980 it was noted by Parker that,

> adoption has seldom been considered as one of the possible futures
> for the child in protracted care. Many social workers seem

distrustful of its finality, some doubt their own capacity to achieve it and are particularly cautious because of the risks of failure. Of all the options indeed adoption seems most often to be measured against a yardstick of near perfection. By contrast, the risk of failure in foster care is more readily accepted.

(Parker, 1980, p. 127)

Given what we know about children's needs and the legal security which adoption affords, we should be asking ourselves some honest and searching questions about why this option is 'seldom' considered. Some social workers may prefer to leave the decisions to foster parents, suggesting that under Section 29 of the 1975 Children Act, those who have continuously cared for a child for at least five years may apply to adopt without fear that the child will be removed from their care before an adoption hearing. Such an attitude cannot but reflect a worrying abdication of responsibility and avoidance of making decisions on the part of individuals who have a professional duty not to opt out of difficult choices.

Using family resources effectively also presupposes planning and placing children with foster or adoptive parents who will work, with others, towards a jointly agreed outcome. In this connection Parker refers to two categories of foster care, of which 'one would aim to provide *alternative* temporary care, the other prolonged *substitute* care, possibly leading to custodianship or adoption'. As he points out, 'something of this kind already exists with the distinction between short- and long-term fostering. But this suggestion does turn upon our ability to assess accurately future prospects' (Parker, 1980, p. 86). Having established the choices which social workers will inevitably have to confront, we may now go on to consider the preparation of family resources and moving into placement.

4

Parents and Children

And one day he said to me: 'You ought to make a beautiful drawing, so that the children where you live can see exactly how all this is. That would be very useful to them if they were to travel some day.'

Antoine de Saint-Exupery, *The Little Prince*

Introduction

I have already referred to the importance of speedy rehabilitation for children who come into care and to the crucial nature of planning in this context. If children are placed with foster parents the latter must be adequately prepared and kept fully informed, in order to facilitate continuing contact between children and their parents and to effect the successful outcome of rehabilitation plans. It is beyond the brief of this book to look in any detail at social work with the families of children coming into care. However, it should be said that we cannot expect children to return home if we do not, first, help parents to modify whatever factors lead to an admission to care; secondly, facilitate continuing contact with their children; and thirdly, provide whatever support is necessary to maintain children with their families. These remarks, of course, beg the question of how often children come into care when sufficient social work and other resources may have been effective in avoiding family breakdown and separation. This question relates not only to day-to-day availability of resources, but also to political and economic circumstances which may influence how far families are able to cope with social and financial demands. In discussing work with biological parents of children in care, where an adoption plan has been made, I must assume that intensive and consistent efforts have been directed at achieving rehabilitation and that a decision has been reached on the basis of the 'welfare principle'.

Working with parents of children in care

While rehabilitation is being actively pursued, social workers and parents should regularly and frequently make a joint assessment of progress. If an agreed plan is interrupted, for example, by parents' failure to visit or maintain contact with their children, the reasons for this must be explored. Lack of confidence, feelings of failure, foster parents' attitudes, misunderstandings, and a variety of other factors, may account for an inability to stick to agreed arrangements. In such cases attempts should be made to remove or at least modify the barriers which inhibit co-operation. It may be the case that despite intensive explanation, planning and support, parents avoid tackling the difficulties which stand in the way of rehabilitation. They may disappear for periods, continue to set up casual and unstable relationships, be more concerned about their own needs than those of their children, be unable or unwilling to develop parenting skills, or have characteristics which interfere with their capacity to be 'good enough' parents, for example subnormality or chronic mental illness.

Given all the factors mentioned hitherto, such as the child's age, previous experiences, quality of relationships with parents or caretakers and so on, the implications of a failure to work towards rehabilitation must be discussed with parents when it becomes apparent that children's and parents' needs are beginning to diverge and time is running out. This discussion must be explicit. I suspect that there is a temptation to 'soften the blow' by leaving options open, suggesting that children should stay where they are 'for the time being' saying that children should remain with their foster parents 'but we will see what happens', or simply not initiating contact with parents on the grounds that this is less painful for them, and incidentally, will avoid 'rocking the boat'.

Any decision to abandon active work towards rehabilitation must be fully explained to parents. If they have been involved in planning, explanations will be based on what parents already know, whether or not they are able and willing to accept this. Discussion should cover three major areas. First, an assessment of how and why parents have not co-operated with the rehabilitation programme and an *evaluation* of why they failed or were unable to do so. If, for example, parents did not visit their children because their own needs took precedence, then this must be pointed out. Before doing this, social workers must have provided sufficient help and support to have made it realistically possible for parents to achieve certain specified goals. There is no point in imposing inappropriate expectations about travelling, number of contacts with children, ability to make and organise plans, social competence, and then reassessing decisions because parents have deviated from the programme.

Secondly, and although this may not be possible in all cases, social workers must explain children's developmental needs and face parents with the difficulties which are likely to be experienced by their children if adequate stability, continuity, and learning opportunities are not provided for them. I have certainly come across parents whose own disrupted backgrounds and lack of rewarding family interaction make them acutely aware of problems for their own children, and well able to understand the possible consequences of failing to meet their needs. The language used and information imparted must be geared to parents' ability to understand. Complicated concepts and jargon must be eschewed in favour of concrete illustrations and explanations which relate to the day-to-day experience of parents. I am not only referring here to language in the sense of vocabulary and sentence construction, but to the social basis of interpretation and the meaning which is assigned to verbal and non-verbal exchanges. The message must *not* be that parents (other than in particular instances which will be discussed later) do not love or care about their children, but that their own needs or difficulties make them impatient, angry, unhappy, depressed and so on, so that they cannot translate their love into good parenting. What I have said may be viewed as obvious. However, I suspect that anxiety or lack of time may lead social workers to make an inaccurate assessment of what parents are able to understand, or to resort to professional 'shorthand' for imparting complicated information. Thirdly, social workers should make clear the alternatives which are open to parents to challenge decisions, specifically in relation to legal action.

In addition to the above, social workers must be honest with parents about plans for their children's future. On numerous occasions I have met social workers who are prepared to tell parents that children are being placed 'long term' with foster parents, but who will not make it clear that such placements are intended to be permanent or are made with adoption as the plan. It is quite possible, and not uncommon, for social workers to avoid this task by resorting to lack of control over final decisions (we cannot guarantee that an adoption order will be granted – it is up to the court); suggesting that we should wait and see if the placement is a success (it might always break down and then we will have distressed the parents for no good reason); or it is not us who are making the decision to adopt (we will leave it up to the foster parents). A further anxiety, and a valid one, is that parents may be able to accept fostering and thus leave the local authority with responsibility for children in care, but that any mention of adoption may precipitate legal action and remove safeguards for children who are subsequently returned home. While recognising this concern I believe that it is outweighed by other considerations.

First and foremost, social workers have a responsibility to parents which includes involving them in planning, explaining decisions, and telling them clearly about any proposal for the future of their children. An avoidance of this responsibility is likely to destroy any possibility of trust. Parents may be angry about an expressed intention to work towards adoption, but at least they will understand the position and be aware of their legal rights. Secondly, social workers' decisions must be open to challenge at the point when they are made. It is ethically unacceptable not to afford parents this opportunity, by failing to provide information, fudging round the edges, or making the plea that a decision was never made – it happened by default or through the passage of time. Thirdly, if parents have been given adequate help, and planning has been based on thorough assessment, social workers should be confident about defending their position in court. Fourthly, if parents wish to contest a decision they should be encouraged to do so before a lapse of time has allowed children to become settled in their new families and emotionally attached to psychological parents.

Reactions of parents to information about a permanent placement and adoption will vary enormously. The literature on responses to loss has now been extended and relates to many circumstances of deprivation and separation. Parents may deny the possibility of such a decision, refuse to acknowledge the significance of their own behaviour or other factors which resulted in the plan, avoid talking about the subject, lay the responsibility at their social worker's door, and so on. It is likely that parents who continue to deny either the decision to place their children for adoption, or the validity of factors associated with this, will take little or no positive action to present their own case or their objections to the plan. Parents may miss this phase or quickly move on to feeling angry about the proposals for their children's future. Anger may prompt them to take some action to regain care of their children or it may be expressed by a hostile, or sometimes violent, reaction to social workers, foster parents, their own extended family or spouses, or 'the system'.

As in other situations of loss, parents may attempt to 'bargain' in order to change a decision. Negotiations may take place with social workers or with a court, but are likely to take the form of promising to maintain contact with children, changing lifestyles, modifying relationships, referring to earlier and better parenting. Or, negotiations may be based on threats to take legal action or intimations of parents' own unhappiness, having nothing to live for, feeling rejected and judged by social workers, being unable to care for other children in the family and so on. Some parents may experience a period of depression when social competence, self-confidence and self-esteem become attenuated. They are unable to find rewards in other relationships, and the world appears a hostile and untrustworthy place. Depending on their involvement in planning, their own personalities and experiences, and relationships with social workers, some parents may be able to accept the decision about their children's future. In my experience, it is unusual for acceptance to be expressed at an early stage. However, I have found that on many occasions parents who have denied the validity of decisions, or who have maintained an angry and hostile attitude over a long period, are finally able to accept and sometimes to admit that they are unable (or unwilling) to care for their children. In some instances this recognition may not occur until a few days before an adoption hearing. It may be explicit, or it may take the form of not agreeing to the adoption but failing to contest the application in court. Some parents are able to say, 'I know its the right thing but I just couldn't face it', or, 'While the children were in care they could always have come home – now I'll never have them back.' Parents who reach the stage of acceptance may well experience further depression. A concern for their children's future should not lead us to forget parents' needs or to abandon them once an adoption order has been made.

The phases of denial, anger, bargaining, depression and acceptance will be well known to readers who have looked at literature on dying, bereavement and other forms of loss. They are equally applicable to helping us understand and anticipate the reactions of parents to permanent separation from their children and loss of their parenting role. It should be remembered that these phases are only a useful way of differentiating between types of responses. However, as in other situations involving loss, individuals may not progress consistently from anger to acceptance, but may move back and forth between different phases or adopt a particular attitude which enables them to cope with impending or actual loss. Previous experiences, relationships, and feelings about self and others will also influence the nature of these reactions. One of the difficulties for people who are facing separation and loss is that others will expect certain kinds of reactions and may impose anticipated time limits on working through particular phases. It is essential that social workers should avoid such assumptions about how parents will respond to an adoption plan, or about the possibility for change in their feelings.

We must therefore accept that parents will react in a number of ways to an intended plan to place their children for adoption, that they may move through identified responses to potential or actual loss, or that they may express and maintain a limited range of responses such as denial or anger. Some parents may have been struggling with feelings of guilt and confusion about their inability to relate positively to their children or to fulfil adequately the parenting role. A recognition of these feelings and the removal of impossible expectations of success may come as a relief, and allow parents to relinquish their children for permanent family placement. Social workers must be ready to accept and work with whatever reactions are forthcoming. There is a danger that if parents express denial or anger social workers will withdraw because they consider further discussion to be pointless, fear that it will increase parents' hostility or may encourage them to take legal action, feel that they are causing unnecessary distress or are uncomfortable about their authority to carry out intended plans. It must be recognised that some parents will not perceive social workers as providing acceptable help and will continue to see an adoption plan as a denial of their rights and contrary to their own needs and feelings.

In the context of this discussion, social work with parents of children in care may be viewed as having several components. First, social workers must explain decisions which may have been reached within a local authority structure or through a court. Explanations should not be viewed as 'one-off' exercises, but may need repetition to answer further questions, confirm previous discussions, refer to events preceding certain decisions, and to ensure that parents understand the significance of intended action. Secondly, wherever possible social workers must help parents to distinguish between their competence as parents and their qualities and capabilities as individuals. This can only be achieved through an approach which expresses respect and a willingness to try and understand the feelings and perceptions of parents. Social workers must convey the message that a decision to place children for adoption is not equivalent to branding parents as bad or unacceptable, to a lack of concern for their feelings, or to a withdrawal of help because they are unimportant or undeserving. This message must be supported in practice by continued and reliable opportunities for discussion between social workers and parents.

Thirdly, where appropriate, social workers must make it clear to parents that they still have something to offer their children and that they are not to be dismissed because they cannot fulfil a parenting role. We can point out that children need to know about their parents, backgrounds, and reasons for permanent placement and that histori-cal events and shared experiences will play an important part in how they see themselves and cope with the future. Parents may be encouraged to contribute photographs or information to a life story book, to help in planning their child's move to a new family, to explain directly to their child why they feel unable to have him or her home. Fourthly, and in relation to comments above, parents may need reassurance that prospective adopters will attempt to understand their difficulties and reasons for placement, and will handle this information sympathetically when providing explanations to their child. It may be difficult for parents to articulate some of these concerns and it is the social worker's responsibility to recognise their importance, respond to tentative cues from parents, and to make it clear by an attitude of concern and attentiveness that they are available to help parents deal with their worries and feelings as well as to implement decisions regarding their children.

Fifthly, the foregoing discussion presupposes that parents are prepared to accept social work help and to talk about their children's future. However, parents who respond with denial or anger should not immediately be defined as difficult or impossible to work with, and abandoned in favour of more rewarding clients. I can remember one mother whose five-year-old twins were being placed for adoption without her agreement. She consistently denied the validity of this decision, referring to previous housing problems, relationship difficulties, lack of social work support, and numerous other factors beyond her control, which had made it impossible for her to carry out her parental tasks and responsibilities. However, she maintained that all this had changed. She had a new house in a better neighbourhood, a stable (though recent) relationship with her co-habitee, and felt better about her ability as a parent. Although she did not intend to have her children home at the moment she wanted this possibility to remain open so that she could consider it at 'some time in the future'. This mother's first social worker supported the plan for her children's adoption. However, he opted out of working with her and her co-habitee because he felt that continued contact would cause her more pain and any reminder of her inability to care for her children would be brutal. In other words he assumed a 'low profile' or 'lets not rock the boat' approach. A subsequent social worker decided that this mother was being deprived of help, both in her own right, and in relation to accepting the proposals for her children's future. He refused to accept her explanations that events beyond her control had prohibited her from caring for her children, gently presenting the reality of what had actually happened. Her present situation was no better or more amenable to meeting her children's needs than it had been for several years. When this mother concentrated on her own feelings and needs the social worker acknowledged these as important, but also focused her attention on the welfare of her children. It was pointed out that children need parents to care for and look after them on an every-day basis, that she had been unable to do this for a considerable time, and that she was not expressing an intention or wish to do so in the immediate future. After many discussions of this sort and with a great deal of concern and support, the mother agreed to the adoption application.

The social worker was aware that during this process he was opening the way for this mother to feel increasing distress and to come face to face with her perceived failure as a parent. What he did provide, however, was an opportunity for her to do something constructive in terms of her children's welfare, to gain some understanding of her own needs and choices about the future, and to have some control over the final outcome. Neither did the social worker abandon the mother when she had agreed to adoption, but continued to help her deal with the sadness which this decision entailed. In the long run this mother had experienced a positive relationship with her social worker, had been able to perceive his concern for her as well as for her children, and had developed some sense of self-esteem through an increasing understanding of her children's needs and participation in planning for their future.

Some parents will only be able to deal with permanent separation from their children by continuing a pattern of denial or anger. Every effort should be made to help parents move on from this position. If social workers withdraw from parents this should be on the basis that they are unable or unwilling to modify their perceptions or to change their pattern of coping. Premature closure of work with parents is likely to confirm their view that social workers are only interested in 'taking their children away', or to increase their sense of hostility, isolation and anger that no one cares about their feelings once they have 'got their children in care'.

In these situations the decision is sometimes made to allocate different social workers to parents and children. Two arguments are usually adduced in favour of this approach. First, that parents may be able to accept help more readily from a social worker who was not involved in separating them from their children. Secondly, that it is difficult for social workers to reach a decision about placing children for adoption when they have a sympathetic relationship with the parents and do not feel able to cause them distress or endanger opportunities for providing further help. These arguments may be valid in some circumstances. Whenever possible, however, I would favour the same social worker maintaining a relationship with parents while at the same time working with their children. This is likely to facilitate more effective communication, to help parents keep a link with their children, and to demonstrate that the person who is responsible for their children's future well-being is also concerned about their welfare and feelings.

Working with parents wishing for adoption

Some parents will be considering the possibility of adoption for their children in advance of their birth and subsequent placement with prospective adopters will be arranged with parents' agreement. In other instances parents may have felt ambivalent about keeping their babies, but find that they are only able to decide on adoption when their children are months or even a few years old. A mother who wanted her two-year-old son to be placed for adoption explained that initially she had been unable to obtain an abortion. She had later approached an adoption agency but finally accepted the advice of family and friends that she would grow to love her baby, that she would always regret 'giving him up', that other people would think her callous and uncaring if she went ahead, and so on. For two years she had attempted to lead the kind of life she wanted, feeling increasingly guilty about leaving her son with different caretakers and painfully aware that he was the focus of her resentment and frustration. In the end she came to a difficult decision on her own and urgently needed the acceptance, understanding and continuing support of her social worker.

Another mother felt unable to ask for adoption for her twelve-month-old baby until a social worker recognised her fear of being judged as indifferent and abnormal. Her baby was continually admitted to hospital for minor complaints and investigation of his failure to thrive. Doctors were concerned that shortly after each admission this apathetic and physically poorly developed child began to flourish in his clinical surroundings. When asked if she found it hard to look after her child, this mother was able to talk about her confused and unhappy feelings. The baby's father was violent and uncaring towards her, she had tried to pretend she was not pregnant, had feared the birth, and had never enjoyed or felt that she loved her child. There was no one to talk to about her feelings and anyway it all went to prove that she was a bad person and must be 'peculiar' if she was incapable of loving her own baby. Social work help enabled this mother to acknowledge her feelings without being judged, provided reassurance that she was not bad or abnormal, gave her an opportunity to sort out what was best for her and her child's future, and supported her through the eventual choice of permanent separation and adoption.

Work with expectant parents has traditionally followed an established pattern. First, at the pre-birth stage; secondly, following the birth; and thirdly, during the period when a baby has been placed with prospective adopters and until an adoption order is made. Following a baby's discharge from hospital it has been the usual practice to arrange a placement with 'pre-adoption' foster parents until the baby is six weeks old. At this time the baby will have a medical examination and will subsequently be placed with prospective adopters, in whose continuous care he or she must remain for at least three months before an adoption order can be made. It would be tedious and probably not very helpful to spell out the statutory requirements for an adoption placement. These are covered by the 1958 Adoption Act, the 1975 Children Act and the Adoption Agencies Regulations.

At the time of writing the Department of Health and Social Security is revising the Adoption Agencies Regulations, as this statutory instrument has not been substantially modified since its introduction and fails to accommodate changes in practice. The Children Act is also undergoing a phased implementation. However, excellent summaries and explanations of the law may be found in Holden (1982) and ADSS (1976). A mother, and where legally necessary a father are not, at present, permitted to sign an agreement to adoption until their baby is six weeks old. This period is designed to allow time for a mother to recover from the birth, and to further consider her feelings once the baby has assumed a 'real' and individual existence. A pre-placement medical examination at six weeks has also been seen as offering greater assurance to prospective adopters that their baby will be physically and mentally healthy. Once parents have signed their agreement to adoption and the application papers are received by a court, any change of mind cannot result in the return of their baby unless by leave of the court. Prospective adopters are therefore afforded additional security once the baby is six weeks old and agreement to adoption has been given.

Before the baby is born

As many social workers will know, pre-birth work is often carried out only with prospective mothers. Where the baby will be illegitimate a relationship with the father may have been discontinued or may have been transient, or of little significance in the first instance. Generally speaking, the fathers of illegitimate babies are afforded relatively little social or legal attention. They may apply for custody but their agreement to adoption is not required. However, we should employ the principle that wherever possible, and if acceptable to both parties, social work help should be made available to mothers and fathers of babies who may be placed for adoption. This is desirable because, however the situation is legally defined, both are parents of the expected child and there is no good reason to *assume* that fathers do not have views about their children's future. A concern to involve both parents in planning may also avoid difficulties later on when aggrieved and neglected fathers may decide to apply for custody. However unlikely the success of such an application, it will introduce tension and uncertainty into an already painful and distressing process for some mothers, may hold up permanent placement for children, and, depending on timing, may interfere with the commitment and emotional attachment of prospective adopters with whom babies are already placed. During the forthcoming discussion I will refer to work with mothers, because in practice this may often be the focus of social workers' attention. My comments should, however, be understood to refer to fathers whenever it is possible to involve them.

The first reaction to a confirmed pregnancy, especially for young women living at home with their parents, is likely to be one of denial or panic. In some cases denial may be maintained by avoiding emotional attachment to an unborn child, failing to seek or accept social work help, or staying away from ante-natal services. In extreme circumstances women may put off having a suspected pregnancy confirmed, leaving little time for sorting out feelings and possible courses of action before the baby is born. Social workers may thus encounter continued denial. They must also remember that many women are likely to employ denial at various times, as is to be expected in any situation where people are faced with impending separation and loss. Responses like, 'I don't want to think about it now', 'It doesn't feel real', 'I'll talk about it nearer the time', are not uncommon. Feelings of panic may also lead women to avoid thinking about important issues, because they fear the responses of parents or boyfriends, are unable to sort out or accept their own mixed reactions, and cannot order or assess the possibilities which may be open to them.

Social workers can help in several ways during this period. First, when women may be feeling confused, guilty, ashamed and unable to get their thoughts in any kind of manageable order, social workers should respond with an attitude which is non-judgemental, accepting, and introduces some stability into what probably appears a thoroughly disorganised world. Secondly, social workers can provide order by helping women to break down a complicated, and for some, a potentially overwhelming problem into smaller parts which may then be realistically tackled. Such analysis is basic to much social work intervention and must precede assessing possibilities for action and deciding upon priorities.

The process of analysis is likely to continue throughout work with women and will enable discussion about the following questions. How do I feel about the expected baby? Are these feelings related to the circumstances of conception, to the nature of my relationship with the father, to a judgement about my own behaviour, or to the reaction of others? What are the practical constraints which will influence subsequent decisions? Is there room at home for the baby, who will look after him/her while I go out to school or work, what kinds of difficulties or tensions is this likely to promote given the family's situation and attitudes, will I get the necessary support, do I want to leave home and am I capable of managing on my own, how will I cope financially, what are the community resources open to me? What are my future plans? Do I want to go on to further education, what will be my feelings about being tied down to caring for a child, will I resent my lack of freedom, am I ready to get married, will I be able to have other children later on? What will people think of me if I place my child for adoption or how will they react to me as an unmarried mother? How do I know that other people will bring my child up with the kind of love and care that I would want and what will they tell him or her about me? How will my child understand the decision to give him or her up and what will they think of me? These are only the obvious and major questions and there are many more.

Depending on the situation, questions will be more or less significant and amenable to finding answers. For some women, practical constraints and expectations about the future may render decision-making about adoption a relatively clear, if not a painless, matter. However, as should be apparent from the foregoing list, relevant questions cover a wide range of financial and practical issues as well as subtle and often ambivalent areas of feeling. For this reason a social worker's ability to order and analyse complex and related topics is vital in helping parents to plan for the future. Thirdly, it is important for parents to understand what adoption actually means in terms of permanent and legal separation. Social workers may need to go over this ground on several occasions both before and after a baby's birth. In order to ensure that this work is done the Adoption Agencies Regulations require that parents should be given an adoption memorandum, that this should be explained to them, and that they should indicate in writing that they have understood the contents. The memorandum sets out the implications of adoption, outlines Section 26 of the 1975 Children Act (access to birth records), and summarises the legal position, including giving agreement to adoption and the grounds on which a court may be asked to dispense with parents' consent. It should be made clear to parents that signing the memorandum does not constitute an agreement to adoption. Confusion and anxiety may make it difficult for parents to grasp this information and reassurance should be given that the social worker will be available to answer questions and provide further explanation as time goes on. Fourthly, women may be worried about what will happen when the baby is born; what will people think, how will they feel, will they have to look after the baby, what will they say to other mothers, will they be given time to think over their decision, and so on. Social workers should confirm that arrangements may be made for women not to see or care for their babies if this accords with their feelings at the time.

Some social workers consider that immediate separation of mothers and babies is unhelpful because it may reinforce denial, allow mothers to avoid making an active decision, and impede the expression of grief and process of mourning for a 'lost' baby. It is appropriate for social workers to explain this view to women and to help them anticipate problems which might arise if they do not see their babies. However, a social worker's task is not to make decisions *for* a mother, but to help her consider available options and possible consequences. Continuing support must be emphasised and mothers reassured that their social worker will see them shortly after the birth. It must be understood that mothers will be allowed time, an opportunity to explore their feelings, and help in making their own decisions. Social workers should convey an appreciation that mothers may feel differently after a birth, that this is acceptable, and that they will not be condemned as 'fickle' or 'time-wasters' if they decide against adoption.

Fifthly, at least some of the difficulties experienced by pregnant women are likely to be exacerbated by family and friends. This pressure may be particularly intense for young women living at home with their parents. Just like their daughters, parents will have to cope with mixed feelings both about the pregnancy and about their role in educating, socialising and understanding their children. Reactions of shock, shame, and guilt will be related to questions such as, where have we gone wrong; why didn't we see it coming; how could she do this to us; what will everyone say? Some parents will respond to their dilemma and confusion by trying to make decisions for their children and suggesting single solutions such as adoption. Others may deny any responsibility for what has happened and demand that their daughters leave home. Whatever the nature of parental reactions, youngsters will need social work help to consider all the possibilities which are open to them and which their parents may be unwilling to recognise or to discuss. Parents may be so bound up with their own feelings and anxieties that communication among family members becomes distorted or breaks down.

Social workers should thus be prepared to work with families by understanding their confusion and distress, helping them to assess and analyse the problem, facilitating communication by encouraging the expression of feelings and views within the safe boundaries of external control, and making time available for parents to talk about their disappointment, sense of failure and ideas about the future. It is important for some parents to know that social workers are concerned about their feelings as well as those of their children. Social work help in maintaining open communication may make the difference between constructive and mutually supportive interaction between family members or the development of destructive relationships based on resentment, blame, anger and increasing social and emotional distance. Throughout a pregnancy there may be much well-intentioned but conflicting and sometimes misguided advice, which will be offered from all directions. Continuing social work support and acceptance should help families to concentrate on their own feelings, needs, and available options, when confronted with the expectations and opinions of well-meaning advisers.

When the baby is born

Work carried out before a baby is born should have considered alternatives for the future, helped a mother and her family to understand their present feelings and to anticipate possible reactions to the birth, and maintained mutual support and open communication. This is only the groundwork. Social workers must be ready to help parents and their families to reassess the situation if their feelings change when the physical and emotional impact of a baby becomes real and unavoidable. Some previous work may be repeated on a different basis; rethinking alternatives, working out the implications and consequences of a desired option, making practical plans, and analysing complicated and confusing feelings.

It is at this stage that mothers may need immediate and consistent support, since they may be emotionally vulnerable, surprised by their own reactions, and under pressure to take a particular course of action. Expectations may be presented in a subtle form by the disapproving attitudes of nursing staff who know about an adoption plan, the questioning glances of other mothers, an intimation of irresponsibility, disappointment in the faces of visiting friends and relatives. Or opinions may be directly conveyed by nurses or other patients who make comments like, 'I don't know how any mother could give her baby away, you don't know what you will be missing; you will regret it when it's too late; every baby needs its mother'. Although not intended to do so, such remarks reinforce feelings of guilt, anxiety and fears about the future. They also incorporate an assumption that the wish for adoption derives from mothers' lack of concern, selfishness and callous ability to 'offload' their children onto other people. Social workers should help mothers to maintain a sense of confidence and self-esteem, and continue to focus attention on an assessment of their needs when they may feel pushed in all directions by competing expectations and demands.

If a mother decides to keep her baby, the social worker may be required to help family members understand and come to terms with the position, and to provide practical and financial advice. In other circumstances, arrangements would be made for babies to be moved to pre-adoption foster parents, until joining prospective adopters at about six weeks old. Mothers may see this time as representing final separation and begin to pick up activities and plans without reference to their babies. However, for some mothers a period of pre-adoption fostering may provide an opportunity to explore the realistic possibilities of caring for their children and reassessing their feelings about parenthood. Visiting and handling their babies in the foster home will be essential if they are planning to assume a parenting role, and may be helpful for those mothers who have ambivalent feelings about their children. Throughout this period social workers should maintain the kind of approach already outlined. A few mothers may remain ambivalent and unable to make a decision. It may therefore be necessary to reinforce information about children's developmental needs and to point out that the longer a baby remains with foster parents, the more likely it is that significant emotional attachments will be developed with them.

Placement with prospective adopters

Social workers should be aware that reactions to loss will vary. Some mothers who place their babies for adoption will have a clear idea of their future and may feel little more than relief that they are now free to get on with their lives. In these circumstances it may be other members of a family who are shocked, upset, and disappointed, and who need social work help in understanding and accepting decisions regarding adoption. However, some mothers will experience a period of grief and mourning, and relatives or friends may be unable or unwilling to help them work through this. Social workers must let mothers know that it is acceptable and normal for them to talk about their babies and to go over, and confirm, their reasons for choosing adoption. It is difficult for mothers to do this if others are hostile, angry, or confused about their decision. If mothers are under pressure to keep their babies they are likely to be afraid of expressing ambivalent feelings or sadness. Literature on separation and loss suggests that 'grief work' can only be successfully accomplished through an ability to recognise the reality of loss, to talk about the lost object, and to accept feelings of sorrow, despair and meaninglessness.

At some stage social workers will be compiling written information for prospective adopters. This should include information about the mother (physical appearance, personality, interests) and about the father wherever possible; details of the birth (place, time, baby's weight, any special factors); reasons for placement, characteristics of mother's and father's family and personal history. For some mothers, participation in this exercise will be important as a way of showing their concern, explaining their decision, and recognising the reality of loss. If mothers wish to write a letter for the adopters or for their child, to provide photographs, or to send a present which will accompany their baby into the adoptive home, then they should be encouraged and helped to do so. Adequate preparation and support of prospective adoptive parents should enable them to accept and to use positively such background information and links with their new child's past. Mothers who do not wish to co-operate in providing this information should be helped to understand the importance of such knowledge for their children's future welfare, and social workers should make it clear that, in any event, they will be writing as full an account as possible for prospective adoptive parents. Finally, social workers must be prepared to accompany mothers (and where appropriate fathers) to sign their agreement to adoption. They should not withdraw automatically when an adoption order is made, unless it is clear that their help and support is no longer needed.

Some general comments

Before concluding this section, we should take account of three further points. First, a period of pre-adoption fostering and a full medical examination at six weeks old has traditionally preceded placement with prospective adopters. The desirability of this practice has been questioned, and it is now not unusual for babies to be placed with prospective adopters immediately on discharge from hospital. Any decision to make a 'direct placement' must rest upon a mother's readiness to reach a conclusion about her baby's future. Having decided to place their children for adoption many mothers are anxious that they should be able to settle down with their new parents as soon as possible. This prevents an additional move for babies and enables prospective adopters to begin developing attachments at the earliest possible opportunity. One word of caution should be added here. I have met some mothers who have consistently denied their feelings, and the request for a direct placement may reflect a continuation of this denial. Social workers must be alert to this possibility, and if necessary let mothers know that pre-adoption fostering is considered essential for them to recognise, accept and consider the implications of their situation.

Secondly, it is important to offer mothers some control over what is happening. This may be achieved by helping them to think about the kind of families they would like for their children, encouraging them to participate in compiling information, and facilitating a meeting with prospective adopters if they request this. Such meetings enable mothers to explain their reasons for placement to prospective adopters, and are usually viewed as helpful by the latter who feel that first-hand knowledge will assist them with subsequent explanations to adopted children. Mothers and prospective adopters will probably want social work support when the meeting takes place and this should be made available. Although these occasions are usually emotional and sometimes painful, in my experience mothers and prospective adopters have never regretted meeting. They have often felt reassured by seeing and talking to each other as human beings with many shared hopes, anxieties, disappointments, and a common concern for a particular child's welfare. Frequently they are able to develop and express a sympathetic awareness of each other's feelings which, as research has indicated, will be helpful to adopted children as they are maturing and coping with explanations about their adoption and background.

Thirdly, as is generally the case, social work intervention will only be useful and appropriate if it is responsive to clients' needs and is not a reflection of our own expectations and values. This basic premise means that social workers must be alert to how others perceive their difficulties and accept their interpretation of reality as a starting point for interaction. In many instances, where family and friends quite naturally proffer advice or make demands, social workers may be the only available people who will listen, attempt to understand, and facilitate decision-making on the basis of the fullest possible information. This is not to overlook that our statutory duties may sometimes conflict with clients' perceived needs and wishes, but to appreciate that we should begin by trying to grasp the significance of the client's world as it appears to him and be clear about the reasons for any subsequent divergence in assessment or decisions.

Working with children

The idea that children should know about, and be helped to understand, their personal history is now familiar and apparently acceptable. It has gained prominence through research, the kind of debates about 'genealogical bewilderment' to which I have already referred, and its recognised significance for the development of identity and self-esteem. The growing pressure to give a voice to children in care has used the moral language of personal and social rights to define their participation in planning, control over their future, and access to historical and present information about themselves and significant others. This view is clearly set out in the BASW Charter for Children (BASW 29/3/1977). The same approach is applicable in the context of adoption, or for that matter, in any form of placement with a substitute family. Where babies are being placed for adoption, the Adoption Agencies Regulations require specific written information to be given to prospective adopters.

As I have shown, this account should be extended to include both facts and qualitative observations about biological parents and their decisions to place for adoption. Photographs, gifts, and other mementos, may also be included in the historical package. I have found, that given adequate preparation, prospective adopters are able to maintain this historical continuity by adding photographs of the hospital where a baby was born, pre-adoption foster parents, social workers, the court where an adoption order was granted and so on. If a mother has named her baby, prospective adopters are often keen to include this, possibly as a middle name, so that their adopted child will know that he or she has a name given by biological and adoptive parents. Before such attention was focused on this topic we may have been guilty of assuming that older children understood what had happened to them, that dwelling on the past would have been dangerous, or that given the possibility of a happy and settled future the experiences of a troubled history could be safely left behind. However, the growing practice of placing older children in permanent substitute families has concentrated attention on a child's need for preparation. It is argued that the skill and commitment of substitute parents should not be considered sufficient to help children who remain confused and angry about what has happened to them or who perceive themselves as bad, blameworthy, destructive, and unlovable because of previous experiences. If permanent placements are intended to safeguard a child's future, it is negligent to allow children to move into new families without adequate preparation.

What should be done?

Working with children, in the context of our discussion, covers three major areas. First, children who have spent a considerable period in care and have probably experienced many moves, are likely to be confused about the chronology and content of their biographies. There may be gaps in memory, and children who have lost contact with parents and significant others may have little sense of continuity and a minimal or fantasised conception of their families of origin. Many of us will have hazy or incomplete memories of our childhood years, but we usually have access to sources of information or artefacts which provide us with links to the past. Many children in care do not have these resources or are not sufficiently independent to make their own inquiries or to seek out relevant knowledge. There are likely to be many questions which must be tackled including those relating to birth information, parents and other family members, reasons for coming into care, previous placements, significant caretakers, and why and how decisions have been made. Clearly, every child in care should have an understanding of his or her biography. It is suggested that those who will be moving into permanent family placements cannot achieve a future-oriented sense of security while their history remains unclear or unknown.

Secondly, children may carry over feelings from past separations or painful experiences which may be distorted and are likely to influence present behaviour and the ability to accept new relationships. A number of examples come readily to mind. A six-year-old girl was referred for family placement. She had been emotionally and physically neglected by her immature and unsupported mother and was placed with childless foster parents when she was two years old. As she grew older her tantrums and stubborn defiance began to grate on her pleasant, quiet, and even-tempered foster parents. Two natural-born children subsequently arrived in this family. Differences in personality and demands for attention led to the foster child being gradually pushed out to the boundary of family interaction where warmth, closeness and emotional rewards were virtually non-existent. She reacted with greater demands for attention and the placement disrupted. This little girl was removed and with little reference to what had happened was rapidly placed with a couple who had an older daughter. Two major themes emerged. First, our little girl could not bear to have babies in the house and continually threatened and bullied the couple's natural born daughter. Secondly, she spent her time running away, walking around in circles pinching and smacking herself with the words 'you are a bad, naughty girl', or setting up destructive situations and then promptly packing her bags in readiness to leave. These responses to her previous experience need little interpretation, and despite nearly two years of real affection and commitment from her new foster parents she was unable to believe that she was not bad and unlovable and that the previous rejection was not totally her fault.

Alternatively, we could consider the nine-year-old boy whose foster placement broke down after three years. His foster home had been a quiet, well-regulated household where voices were infrequently raised and strong feelings were kept subdued. No one ever talked about why he was in care or why he never saw his biological parents. This child had been emotionally rejected by his foster family for a long time before he was rapidly moved on to another family placement, after only a couple of months in residential care. Children's home staff reported that he had been well behaved and shown no signs of sorrow or anger over his separation from the foster family. Shortly after joining his new foster parents his anger erupted. He physically attacked his foster mother, pushed her down the stairs, said he would kill her, and finally out of control collapsed in desperate but tearless sobs. Then there was the twelve year old who had been in a children's home since coming into care eighteen months before placement with a new family. His parents did not want to see him or to talk about his future, but they were unable to tell him that they had refused to consider his return home. He accused his foster parents of keeping him away from loving parents who wanted him back, rejected any requests on the grounds that his foster parents had no right to make them and did everything he could to disrupt the placement.

I'm sure readers are aware of many children who carry a mistaken or distorted sense of responsibility for separation or rejection, or who translate their experiences with uncaring or incompetent parents into warm and loving memories because it is all they have to hang on to. Children in this position are unable to develop a well-balanced sense of their own identity, to grasp the important fact that all people are both good and bad, strong in some respects and vulnerable in others, and to believe in their own goodness and ability to give and to receive affection. If children take confusion, anger, or unrealistic attachments into placements, they and their new families will be at an immediate disadvantage which we probably could have avoided.

Thirdly, we cannot expect children to develop relationships with new parents if they are shuttled into family placements with little understanding of why they cannot return to their biological parents, a resistance to moving into strange and potentially risky situations, or inappropriate expectations of family life. This means that we must not only involve them in planning and decision-making about the future, but must work with them towards family placement and help them to understand why their parents are unwilling or unable to have them home. I know a social worker who had worked long and painstakingly at this process. While the child was being introduced to permanent substitute parents he asked the social worker whether his mother had asked how he was getting on. The social worker replied, 'No, Stephen, but you didn't really expect her to did you?' A brutally honest answer, certainly, but a confirmation of what this child already knew to be the case and a continuing attempt to free him to make a rewarding relationship with new parents.

Some social workers avoid involving children in plans for family placement because they are afraid that children will feel hurt and further rejected if a family cannot be found. Countering this position Curtis suggests that, 'I believe there is nothing more frightening to a child than to feel that someone is making plans about his life over which he feels he has no control. This brings far greater stress to the child than the disappointment of not finding a family, providing that from the beginning, you are totally honest about the difficulties of finding parents for children (Curtis, 1983, p. 45). Curtis explains the visual aids which are used to help children understand the process of finding and preparing families, what happens when people are meeting and trying to get to know each other, and the hard work, mutual adjustments, and 'ups and downs' of family life.

How should we do it?

I have already referred to the use of life story books which build up a picture of a child's biography using words, maps, charts, family trees, pictures, photographs, or indeed any form of presentation or material which will help children of different ages to grasp the chronology and content of their lives to date. However, before we can begin working with children in any way which is acceptable to them, we must engender an atmosphere in which we listen carefully to children and are prepared to respond not only to explicit, but sometimes to subtle or ambivalent cues. It is possible to miss or to avoid children's messages in children's homes where there are many demands for attention, or in any situation where we are not prepared to hear them or fear getting ourselves into deep water. Questions may be presented in a tangential way, remarks may be made when we are going through the door, comments may be directed at teddy bears or dolls, and confusion or anger may be acted out in play. If we are not listening and watching carefully, if we respond to a tentative probe with 'I'm too busy now, that's all in the past, don't worry about that – it will only upset you, cheer up – every thing will be all right', or if we avoid opportunities to share sadness and grief, children will cease to trust us and may feel unable to make another approach.

A life story books is perhaps the most basic and concrete way of structuring work with children. It should be remembered, however, that an historical record is likely to involve painful and sometimes unacceptable periods in children's lives. They may reach a point which they feel unable to tackle and to which they will need to return later on. During the course of this work separations and rejections must be explained. If children have never been able to express their grief or anger they should be encouraged and allowed to do so, with the knowledge that this is acceptable and that their worker will not reject or abandon them. Children who carry the burden of responsibility for previous rejections or who think themselves bad and unlovable must be helped to work out what actually happened, why people felt and behaved as they did, and what part they realistically played in these situations. Life story books cannot be viewed as simple chronological accounts but must also provide opportunities for understanding as well as describing the past, and allowing children to express their feelings in a safe and accepting relationship.

Clearly not all children are either old enough or emotionally capable of using language or direct conversation to express their feelings. In most instances social workers will need to forget about the formal interview and 'grown-up' forms of social exchange. Some children who cannot face very painful parts of their background will be unable to talk about themselves as having had these experiences, but may be prepared to express memories and feelings through the relatively safe medium of a doll or puppet. There are many ways of allowing children to 'talk' about the past and present, without specific reference to themselves through painting and play.

Similarly, children who have limited linguistic and conceptual skills will need concrete illustrations of ideas, like giving and receiving love, making relationships, loss and separation. Communication can be encouraged through writing 'pretend' letters or using toy telephones. A colleague recently told me about a six-year-old girl he had been working with. Her mother had chosen to continue living with a man who had sexually assaulted herself and her sister. Relationships with her mother had in any event been chronically distorted, and as there appeared to be no possibility of rehabilitation in the near future, plans had been made for permanent placement with a substitute family. This child felt that it was her fault that she had been 'sent away', refused to believe that her mother had made it impossible for her to return home, and insisted on different occasions that her mother's co-habitee had either disappeared or was a 'good man' who had really loved and cared for her. Through play she had been able to grasp the reality of what had happened but could not transfer this to her own experience. My colleague reported that the little girl finally said she would phone up 'that mummy' and ask her when she could go home. This she did on the toy telephone and after some minutes of pretend conversation she put down the receiver. She was asked gently what had happened and replied with a combination of anger and sadness that mummy had hung up on her. As my colleague said, having reached the point of bringing this child to recognition, he hardly knew how to respond. His immediate reaction was to provide comfort and reassurance, after which he was faced with the painful task of helping this little girl express her grief and move on to form new attachments.

I have only referred to the principles of this kind of work since a detailed description warrants a book in itself. However, there are now some excellent and highly readable accounts which cover methods of working and provide the support and encouragement of individual workers' attempts to grapple with this difficult and highly charged area of intervention. References will be found in the Guide to Further Reading.

Should we do it?

This may seem like a strange question given the discussion above. However, it is sometimes more effective to establish the case for doing something and then to deal with worries and objections. A residential social worker recently phoned me, ostensibly to thank me for some literature on life story book work with children. Having conveyed her thanks she hesitated and there was clearly something else that she wanted to say. With a little prompting she explained that she was getting ready to begin a life story book with a ten-year-old boy who had been in care for six years and who had no contact with his parents. By way of preparing the ground she had asked him if he ever wondered why he was in care and why he never saw his parents. To her alarm he came out with a torrent of destructive abuse towards his parents, herself and anyone else he could think of, and finally gave way to uncontrolled sobbing which she felt at the time 'went on for hours'. The worker was on the point of losing her nerve; she had felt powerless to help this child, responsible for causing him pain, ashamed that she had not been aware of his unhappiness, upset by her own fear and confusion, and had been discouraged from continuing by other staff who saw this form of intervention as brutal and disruptive. It is probable that in her haste and anxiety this worker had misjudged her starting point; she had not begun by preparing the ground but had plunged straight in to the heart of this child's confusion and anger. Better knowledge and support would have enabled her to tackle the work more slowly, to have proceeded at the child's pace, and to have introduced painful experiences in response to the child's readiness.

It is helpful to remember Donley's comments when she says, 'Assume that any child you are going to work with has some deep concern that has never been adequately understood or answered . . . Understand from the beginning that children in care have been hurt: some part of them has been damaged. Never make the assumption that, because everyone presents this child as untouched and undamaged, he must be that way' (Donley, 1975, p. 20). In other words, be prepared and approach such children with care. However, the expression of strong feelings and experience of pain are the very reasons why this work should be done. We now have enough literature on loss, grief-work, and crisis intervention, and sufficient 'practice wisdom' in this area, to establish that unresolved feelings associated with separation and loss inhibit social competence, may lead to distorted or delayed grief reactions, and are likely to result in increased vulnerability and inability to cope with subsequent crises.

Recently, I came across an article which presented the story of some foster parents whose foster children had been removed from their care. Bearing in mind the possibility of dramatic license, at least one of the reasons for the children's removal had been the foster parents' unwillingness to co-operate in life story book work. They argued that until this work had begun the children had been settled and happy. During the course of sessions with their social worker, the children had become progressively more distressed and their behaviour increasingly difficult to handle. The foster parents considered a life story book to be brutal and unnecessary. Of course, we know nothing about how the social worker prepared the children, approached the task, supported the foster parents, or to what extent she involved them in understanding and coping with the children's reactions. It is unacceptable for workers to breeze in and out of life story book sessions without preparing and supporting every day caretakers who will be left to deal with children's inevitable questions and feelings. However, we must recognise that working with children in this way will involve pain. Grief is painful to those who experience it and to those who must stand by and watch. For some that might mean that the whole matter is best avoided, but for others it indicates that the sooner such work is faced the sooner recovery can be accomplished.

Helping children to recognise and cope with loss, unpalatable information, and painful experiences, puts a heavy burden on workers who must see this through. When a child's world is in disarray it is the worker who must provide continuity, stability, safety and control. No one should begin this process with children unless they can guarantee to be reliable and to stick it out. At the same time children should be able to see their workers as human beings who are capable of feeling and responding to emotions. Neilson says about a worker in this context that, 'If the child is sad, he should comfort him. If he is crying, he should hold him and provide loving comfort until the child is calmed. He should give the child a full measure of time to express his feelings. No child was ever hurt by seeing tears in a worker's eyes, if at the same time he knew that the worker had things under control' (Neilson, 1979, p. 89).

Who should do it?

There may be a tendency to assume that working with children represents such a delicate task that it must only be undertaken by social workers. This assumption must be put on one side. It is essential that whoever undertakes this work should be reliable and able to develop a relationship of trust and confidence with a child. The task must thus be allocated to the most appropriate person irrespective of professional prestige or power to control information. A designated worker must be given access to all available information, time to do the job properly, and adequate support in coping with inevitable setbacks, anxieties, and personal reactions. If a field social worker is involved with a child in residential care or in a foster home, it is essential that caretakers are well prepared and understand a child's likely responses. They should be consulted between sessions in order to keep them up to date with subjects under discussion and enable them to report on a child's reactions and questions. Although there is one designated worker, it must be remembered that children should be viewed in the context of everyday activities and relationships, which continue when the worker has finished a session and left the scene. Sharing information, trust, and co-operation between those who are caring for and working with children, are vital prerequisites for coping successfully with difficulties and helping children towards an understanding of the past.

Conclusion

When talking about adoption there is often an emphasis on the procedure for 'approving' prospective adoptive parents. In this chapter I have attempted to bring together the other, and equally important, parts of the equation – children and their biological parents. I hope that it is clear both from the point of view of good practice and achieving a desired outcome, that we simply cannot afford to neglect the essential nature of thorough work with children and their parents. Neither should we assume that angry parents cannot be helped or that quiet and well-behaved children do not need help. It would be arrogant to suggest that social workers are equipped to resolve all complex and chronic problems with which they are faced and unrealistic to suppose that what they do have to offer will always be acceptable. However, these are not adequate reasons for abandoning parents who object to our decisions or neglecting children who have an uncertain future and a painful, distorted, or forgotten past.

5

Working with Family Resources

'If I ordered a general to fly from one flower to another like a butterfly, or to write a tragic drama, or to change himself into a seabird, and if the general did not carry out the order that he had received, which one of us would be in the wrong?' the king demanded. 'The general or myself?' 'You,' said the prince firmly. 'Exactly. One must require from each one the duty which each one can perform,' the king went on.

Antoine de Saint-Exupery, *The Little Prince*

Some basic premises

The terms 'vetting' and 'selection' are still commonly used when social workers are talking about pre-placement work with prospective foster or adoptive parents: 'assessment' is little better when it is employed to mean the same thing. I have argued that an assessment approach is unacceptable because there are no consistently established criteria against which to measure acceptability, perceived implications of professional status and power inhibit learning and self-assessment in applicants, and the relationship between applicants and social worker is unlikely to be based on trust, honesty and open communication. If this is so, pre-placement work will be characterised by professional distance, doubt, and anxiety, and while social workers end up with little real understanding of applicants' willingness and ability to undertake particular tasks, applicants may feel unable to express their worries or to ask for help at a later stage. What I intend to explore then, is a preparation model, and although the term 'assessment' will be used, it will become clear that such a usage in this context must be sharply distinguished from its relation to vetting and selection. For clarification, the table on pp. 85–6 summarises major elements of assessment and preparation models.

Basically, then, we must devise a way of working which avoids making the procedure for foster and adoption applicants what Kornitzer (1976) has called a 'gruelling experience' and Lambrick (1974) has referred to as 'an ordeal'. The approach must be such that applicants are not focusing their energy and attention on the projection of an acceptable self-image and impression management. In order to achieve this, several principles governing approach and action should inform our work. First, professional distance is counterproductive. Both the attitudes of social workers and the nature of communication which they establish with applicants, will contribute to how far they are viewed as understanding, and being sympathetic to, the needs and aspirations of prospective foster and adoptive parents. If social workers see their task in terms of assessment and selection, they will seek information from applicants as a basis for judging their suitability. Communication is likely to be directed by the social worker. Kadushin has suggested, 'the argument is made that the interviewer cannot expect openness and readiness to share on the part of the interviewee unless he himself sets an example of such openness . . . the social work literature generally counsels against the worker's emotional response in the interview, instead suggesting objectivity and affective neutrality' (Kadushin, 1972, p. 53).

There is evidence to indicate that where the interviewer is open about personal attitudes and experiences, this is likely to encourage greater openness in the interviewee, and that a tendency to make self-disclosures is related to liking, increased openness and the wish to develop a relationship. I am not suggesting that social workers should abandon any distinction between a professional and personal relationship, or forget their responsibility to the agency and the element of authority which this comprises. However, it is likely that a willingness to facilitate discussion, and an input of personal as well as professional attitudes and ideas, will encourage greater openness between social workers and applicants.

Secondly, social workers must enhance the development of trust. Respondents to my own research (Smith, 1980) clearly resented that they were expected to be honest, while social workers wrote secret reports and withheld vital information – for example, the reasons for rejection of an application. Donley (1975) develops this point in discussing the work of 'Spaulding for Children', an American agency specialising in the placement of older and handicapped children. She asserts that mutual trust depends on the willingness of social workers to share information, and prospective adopters are given the total file relating to any child who might be placed with them. This approach is designed to develop a colleague relationship, and avoids treating people 'as if they were rather feeble minded children who must be spoon fed only the palatable parts of a child's life'. Donley recognises that adopters will differ in educational background and that files will vary in the quality and quantity of information which they contain. Social workers will thus need to help in interpreting and assessing the value of available records. Her point, however, is that social workers should not reinforce their professional status and power, or encourage dependency with regard to access to information, decision-making and trustworthiness. Bass (1975) also comments that lack of trust may contribute to poor relationships and inappropriate decision-making. She says,

> another example of the wide gap between agency and family is the lack of trust sometimes revealed in the sharing of significant information. Occasionally sensitive information is withheld on the assumption that the adopting family might react negatively. Value judgements of workers are placed on what is good and what is bad. This technique is morally questionable.
>
> (Bass, 1975, p. 509)

The attitude of social workers is obviously important for enhancing trust, but confirmation is required in *practice*. Agencies operating an adoption service must have an adoption Panel to approve placements. In most cases the Panel is also used to accept or reject applications from prospective adoptive parents, and frequently the Panel's role is extended to consider applications from prospective foster parents. In my view, applicants should be encouraged to participate in the preparation of reports which are submitted to the Panel. Furthermore, in order to reflect the importance of trust in practice, the final reports, including social workers' comments, should be made available to applicants. (I am not neglecting here the confidential nature of references and will deal with this later on.) In two agencies where I have worked this was normal practice, although some social workers felt that it was too difficult for them to share their interpretations and comments with the people about whom they were writing. It *is* difficult, but trust depends on making our observations available and meaningful to applicants and on allowing ourselves to be challenged.

Thirdly, social workers can spend all the time in the world providing information and guidance but this is to little avail if such help is not acceptable. Many of my own respondents commented that 'career social workers' could not understand their feelings and aspirations and were in no position to assess their potential for adoptive parenthood or to tell them how to bring up children. There is some evidence to suggest that relationship satisfaction of interviewees is significantly greater when they perceive the interviewer as being similar in values and lifestyle preferences to themselves (Tessler, 1975). This raises the question of matching social workers and applicants in terms of what Palmer (1973) calls 'exclusive or preferential assignment of certain types of clients to specific types of treatment personnel'. It would certainly be difficult, and not everyone would agree that it would be desirable, to match characteristics of social workers and applicants to foster or adopt. We can make it clear, however, that we are concerned to help applicants consider the additional tasks involved in fostering and adoption and to assess whether they are willing and able to undertake them. It is not our job to tell them what they should or should not do on a day-to-day basis, except, of course, where foster parents are caring for children on behalf of the local authority and certain policies are operative, for example in relation to legitimate punishments.

Thought must also be given to ways of making information more acceptable. I have already mentioned that group discussions are perceived by applicants to emphasise preparation, to stimulate a critical and constructive exchange of ideas, and to provide a supportive environment for learning. The National Foster Care Association has promoted this approach through its work on 'Parenting Plus' teaching materials, which combine a range of methods tailored to adult education. In addition, advice and support from experienced foster and adoptive parents is likely to be acceptable because they have actually 'done the job'. Middlestadt (1978) suggests that adoptive parents have 'knowledge, expertise and natural helping skills' which can be harnessed to help new applicants. Explaining how this worked in her agency she says, 'volunteers did many of the same things that social workers do. They served as resource persons and as co-leaders of discussion in groups; they were involved in the recruitment of adoptive homes and in making decisions on where a child was placed, and they consulted with the agency on adoption policies and procedures' (Middlestadt, 1978, p. 20). The use of experienced resources in this way changes the traditional role of social workers and recognises that they do not hold a monopoly on helping skills or the ability to impart information. We must get off our professional 'high horse' in order to provide effective and acceptable opportunities for learning.

Fourthly, in discussing this topic Braden (1970) has asserted that 'a partnership is indicated – a partnership that can never be truly balanced (as is real friendship) because the power of the worker cannot be ignored'. Clearly we cannot develop the kind of open and honest relationship with applicants which I am recommending if this problem remains influential but unmentioned. The best way to tackle it is to acknowledge that it exists, because social workers *are* responsible for the welfare of children whom they are placing with new families. We can reassure applicants, however, that if it sounds as though they are going to land themselves in deep water by adopting a particular attitude or problem-solving approach, then we will tell them so. Areas of concern will be openly discussed, rather than hidden away in secret reports to which applicants do not have access. Given this kind of discussion it is anticipated that applicants will withdraw if they come to realise that they are unwilling or unable to undertake the tasks being explored. If an application does get to the point of being rejected, then social workers must explain as far as is possible, and having regard to confidentiality of references, why they or the adoption Panel reached this conclusion. The imbalance of power must thus be placed firmly within the context of honesty and accepting responsibility for explaining decisions.

Fifthly, there has been a tendency to lavish many social work hours on prospective adopters while paying relatively cursory attention to pre-placement work with foster parents. In my view, prospective foster and adoptive parents should be approached in the same way, not only because the former may end up with long-term or permanent placements, but because many areas which are covered during preparation are of equal importance to both groups. For example, attitudes to biological parents, responses to neglect or injury to children, and helping children understand and come to terms with confusing and often unhappy backgrounds, are relevant topics for anyone who will be caring for older children. Dealing with the past, reasons for placement, and talking about biological parents, will also be significant areas of concern for those who are adopting babies. Thus, while a particular emphasis may differ between applicants to foster or adopt, generally the work undertaken will be the same. The only variation in procedure which I would support relates to the use of discussion groups. In this instance two types of groups, with distinctive content, would be arranged; one series of meetings for those who clearly intend to adopt babies or toddlers up to about two years old, and a separate series for people who wish to explore the challenges of fostering a range of children or adopting those who are older. Although this age barrier is somewhat arbitrary, it does ensure that couples who meet in groups have some common expectations and areas of interest and that the content of discussion is relevant to their needs.

The first contact

There has been much discussion about the importance of that first contact between clients and the social work services, whether this occurs initially with a switch-board operator, a receptionist, or a social worker. People who get in touch with us about adoption and fostering will have varying perceptions of their inquiry, different anxieties about the likely response, and many questions which need an answer. They may be involuntarily childless couples who have already telephoned countless agencies to be told that lists are closed, they are outside the area, that a waiting period of months or years for a first interview, and they will only be considered if they are prepared to adopt a handicapped, older, or racially different child.

It is not uncommon for the social worker's remarks to be met with a long pause and tears at yet another disappointment. Or callers may have a particular interest in helping children with special needs or offering a service as foster parents. There may be some difficult questions to ask before inquirers are ready to risk any further involvement with an agency. These will include worries like 'I've been divorced, does that matter?', 'I'm single and agencies don't seem to want to know me', 'I'm physically handicapped or have a particular illness, will this exclude me?', 'I've been in trouble with the police, I would rather you said no now than rejected me later on', and so on. If social workers wish to extend knowledge about fostering and adoption, build up good public relations, and ensure that potential family resources are not lost, now is the time to be helpful, patient and welcoming.

My own research indicated two particular areas of concern. Again and again respondents said that social workers were brusque, did not explain the procedure or help applicants to understand what kind of family resources were needed, and that agencies did not provide opportunities for finding out about adoption and fostering or exploring areas of confusion and concern. One respondent expressed the feelings of many others when he said, 'The telephone contact was very offputting. There were a couple of questions about ourselves and then she said, "Well I must say your chances of adopting a white healthy baby are virtually nil." It was up to me to say that we had an open mind about the kind of child we could consider adopting. The response was upsetting and if I hadn't been a social worker myself and got it all worked out before I phoned, the phone would have gone down and that would have been the end of it.' The second major problem was an apparent lack of knowledge about regional resources and adoption agencies, so that people were sent back to agencies where they did not satisfy eligibility requirements, or found themselves going around in circles where every social worker they spoke to suggested that they contact somewhere else. One respondent succinctly remarked, 'There doesn't seem to be much understanding between societies. Nobody seems to know what anybody else is doing.'

Clearly, we cannot help everyone, particularly couples who wish to adopt babies, but we can be sympathetic, understanding and take the time to listen and explain. Similarly, there seems to be no good reason for ignorance about other agencies in the area, or passing the buck. If social workers are perceived as uncaring and unhelpful, then it is these perceptions that we must acknowledge and deal with. Practical assistance is available in the form of the British Agencies for Adoption and Fostering booklet called 'Adopting a Child', which lists adoption agencies and their eligibility requirements, in England and Wales. Childless couples who wish to adopt babies should receive some explanation about the present situation, reasons for fewer babies being referred for adoption, eligibility criteria, and the kinds of children waiting for new families. Social workers must acknowledge the pain, distress and disappointment felt by these couples and it may well be helpful to express their own feelings of inadequacy and powerlessness to help.

What next?

The first contact may indicate that inquirers want to know more about fostering and adoption, or that they wish to explore relevant issues further before making up their minds about what they want to do. Unless there are particular contraindications I have found it helpful to invite couples and their children, where appropriate, to what we call 'open evenings'. These events should be welcoming and informal. To this end, we have regular venues which are readily accessible and where the keynote of physical surroundings is comfort and informality. A list of venues and dates is sent to inquirers so that they do not have to make an appointment, can turn up when they are able, and do not feel that they have committed themselves to further contact if they subsequently decide to withdraw. There has been a tendency to judge commitment by the amount of effort which people will make to find out about an agency's work. I find this suggestion spurious and arrogant. In my view, we should make it as easy and as comfortable as possible for people to learn about adoption and fostering. This means that meetings must be held in the evenings, must be arranged frequently and must be designed in such a way that those who come do not feel they are being given the 'once over', are being lectured, are being talked down to, or are being put off. The object of the exercise is not to send people away feeling depressed and overwhelmed, but to generate a sense of enthusiasm and concern which is based on a realistic appreciation of the challenges and rewards involved in particular tasks.

Assessment/selection and preparation/education approaches to the adoption procedure

Assessment	Preparation

Goals of adoption procedure

(1) To assess applicants' capacity for adoptive parenthood on the basis of a number of desirable attributes, which it is assumed will facilitate successful adoption outcome.	To work with applicants in exploring the nature of adoptive parenthood and helping them to understand their own feelings about this and the difficulties which may arise from the particular demands and strains of the adoptive realtionship.
To select those applicants who are assessed as showing those desirable attributes and to reject those who are considered problematic in this respect.	To help applicants recognise whether they are willing and able to accept adoption and to withdraw voluntarily from the adoption procedure if they decided that this is not the case.
The social worker governs assessment and selection.	The social worker attempts to facilitate the applicants' ability to assess their own motivation, needs, and abilities, and to engage in self-selection on the basis of increased self-awareness and understanding.

Social worker–applicant relationship

(2) Social worker holds power, knowledge, and diagnostic skills, while the applicant has none of these.	Social worker helps applicant to develop and express self-knowledge and understanding, and to use the power of decision-making to continue or to withdraw from the procedure.

Assessment	Preparation
Social worker diagnoses psychodynamic problems and interprets these to the applicants.	Social worker assumes that applicants are able to consciously recognise their own strengths and weaknesses, and encourages them to consider these.
Social worker and applicant have unequal power and expertise in the relationship; social worker is the recognised expert.	Social worker and applicant engage in mutual discussion and exploration of an application. Social worker is available to promote discussion, rather than to give expert opinions.

Method of working

(3) Usually a series of interviews between social worker and applicant. Social worker asks questions and makes interpretations.	Use of discussion group meetings where social worker may introduce topics, guide discussion. Main flow of communication is between applicants within the group.

Difference of perspective

(4) Assessment takes place in the short term. Applicants are selected on the basis of their assessed capacity for successful adoptive parenthood.	It is recognised that assessment for adoptive parenthood at one stage in the applicant's life is insufficient to enable applicants to manage difficulties which may become apparent after placement and legalisation of adoption. Therefore applicants are encouraged to use agency services after adoption to facilitate continuing education.

Information given at open evenings may be divided into three main areas. *First*, we distinguish between different kinds of placements. These are basically *temporary* placements which may be clearly time-limited and short term, or where the duration of a child's stay may be less easy to predict because of legal factors or difficulties in helping parents to work out some of their problems. In any event such placements require foster parents to work towards rehabilitation, with associated tasks of facilitating parental contact, helping a child to understand why he cannot return home immediately and providing day-to-day security while recognising, with the child, that everyone is trying to get things worked out so that he can rejoin his parents. Or, we may be seeking *permanent* placements which, for some older children who have significant relationships with their parents, will involve parental contact, or which may be intended to result in adoption.

In these cases we need foster or prospective adoptive parents who are willing to make a long-term commitment to helping children work through their problems, accepting and helping children to understand the past and reasons for placement, and providing continuous and secure relationships for children who will probably find it difficult to trust adults or to respond to what they are offered. Mention will also be made of other ways in which people can help, for instance, by providing 'Aunt and Uncle' type contacts, helping youngsters who are leaving residential care to move on to independent accommodation, giving breaks to parents of handicapped children. We must make it clear that we will explain the intended outcome of any placement and will support foster or prospective adoptive parents in working with the plan. However, we can only state our intention, for example that a placement should end in adoption, and while every effort will be made to back this up, contrary decisions may be reached as a result of legal action. Foster and prospective adoptive parents need to be reassured that placements are not open to vagaries of arbitrary changes in plan, but they also need to understand that social workers are rarely in a position to give cast-iron guarantees of outcome.

Secondly, information is given about the kinds of children needing family placement. This will vary between agencies and depend on family resources already at their disposal. Characteristics of children for whom foster and adoptive families are needed should be explained; for example, age, handicaps, racial backgrounds, sibling groups, reasons for coming into care, experiences preceding admission, the possibility of residential care or previous foster home breakdowns, and ways in which children may respond to family placement. It is always helpful to illustrate what is being conveyed by the use of concrete examples. Reference should be made to the ways in which children are placed, from short notice/emergency admissions where they may arrive filthy, infested, confused, and distressed, to planned permanent placements following introductions. Note should be taken of the kind of role required for different youngsters. Those placed on a temporary basis need patient and understanding caretakers – they do not need new psychological parents. Permanent placements involve a parenting role, but this will vary between total parental responsibility in adoption, and encouraging attachment to biological parents as significant others in long-term fostering. Teenagers may not be willing or able to accept a parental relationship with their caretakers, but must have people who will stick with them through thick and thin and encourage increasing confidence and independence. Clearly, these different roles should be matched with the needs, motivation and expectations of people who are considering fostering and adoption.

Thirdly, an outline should be given of agency procedure. I stress that we do not think in terms of 'vetting' applicants, but of helping them to assess the kinds of tasks which they are willing and able to undertake. We hope that they will be able to learn about these tasks through open and honest discussion, and we, in turn, will be honest with them if we identify potential problems or attitudes and feelings which we think will land them in difficulty when caring for the kinds of children that we have to place. Although our emphasis is on co-operation and self-assessment, it must be pointed out that the Boarding Out and Adoption Agencies regulations require certain confidential inquiries to be made. Precise references will depend on individual agency policy, but we also ask for three personal referees who know the applicants well and request full medical examinations and reports on the standard BAAF medical form. We explain that the next step will be for couples, and their children if appropriate, to attend four group discussion sessions which aim to consider, in detail, the tasks involved in fostering and adoption and to prepare applicants for coping with some of the sticky situations which they are likely to encounter.

Although some people flinch at the thought of groups, we point out that these sessions are for them to use in any way which they find most helpful – if they want to listen rather than talk, then that is OK with us. The groups also have the safety of structure and specific jobs for participants to do – they are not expected to sit around in uncomfortable silence with a group leader who refuses to help them out! Application forms are not distributed until the last session of group meetings, when those who have come will have a realistic idea of what they are letting themselves in for and will have formed some idea of what they are willing to undertake. Those who subsequently complete application forms will meet individually with a social worker, usually on about five occasions, to discuss in greater depth what kinds of placements would be appropriate for their families, to develop understanding and preparation begun in groups, and to establish a trusting relationship with their worker who will provide support, guidance, and act as a link with the agency as time goes on. Families will be asked to participate in the preparation of a final written document and will be given a copy, so that they can challenge their social worker's perceptions or recommendations if they are unhappy about the contents. We have to be honest and point out that references, by their very nature, must remain confidential. A brief description may be given of how we match children and foster/adoptive parents in planned placements, the arrangement of introductions and decisions about moving in. People will also want to know about approval procedures and the operation and composition of fostering and adoption Panels. Questions must be answered honestly, and an enthusiastic approach will ensure that we, and the people who have come to listen, do not lose sight of the potential satisfaction and rewards as well as the disappointments and sheer hard work.

Open evenings, then, are designed to provide an overview of an agency's need for different kinds of family resources and to give an introduction to the tasks which are involved. A step-by-step approach is emphasised so that people will be able to withdraw at any stage without feeling that they have wasted our time or let us down. Those who come often look pleasantly surprised when we point out that they need to know about our approach in order to decide if they would like to work with us. What is said on this occasion establishes the premise that future work will be based on co-operation, trust and mutual confidence. Because information is copious and complex, written notes are handed out for couples to take away. In addition we provide everyone with the excellent BAAF booklet, 'Meeting Children's Needs through Adoption and Fostering'. Couples are asked to consider the discussion at an open evening and to have a look at the literature before letting us know if they would like to come to group meetings. Some people withdraw at this stage, but those who wish to proceed should be invited to groups as soon as possible. The procedure should comprise a learning *process*, not a series of one-off contacts with weeks of silence in between. If continuity is broken, applicants may think that we are not bothered, and will lose the momentum required for developing discussion and referring back for clarification of comments and ideas.

Group meetings: children with special needs

As has been noted, these are designed as two separate series for couples considering children with special needs and for those who wish to adopt babies. The former type will be considered first. A maximum of seven couples are invited to each series, and as is the case with open evenings, the keynote is comfort and informality. Two group leaders will normally be present. The NFCA 'Parenting Plus' course is based on six sessions, but because of limited time and social work resources we have to cut every series down to four meetings, each session lasting about two and a half hours. Meetings are held in the evenings and at week-ends, all four sessions must be attended, and couples are encouraged to bring their own children if they are old enough to enjoy some of the material. In my view it is impossible to deal with essential issues in anything less than four sessions or the equivalent of at least ten hours. The content of group meetings is as follows:

Session one: setting the scene

(1) *Introduction*. An explanation of overall aims of the meetings, which are generally to help couples consider some of the issues and experiences involved in fostering and adoption, and to explore what these will mean, in order to develop a better understanding of the tasks, problems and rewards which may lie ahead. Films, tapes and worksheets will be used to stimulate ideas and discussion. We emphasise again that we will *not* be taking note of individual reactions, that we do not expect people to make profound comments or behave like amateur psychologists, and that we will not be awarding black marks to those who prefer to listen. We *will* have something to learn from each other and these meetings provide an opportunity to exchange, develop, and generate some new ideas.

(2) *Introducing ourselves*. Participants are asked to interview another member of the group whom they do not know and to jot down some basic information, for example name, job, family details, interests, why they have come to group meetings. Each member then introduces the person they have interviewed to the rest of the group and explains a little about them. This exercise is guaranteed to break the ice, and it is sometimes difficult for group leaders to stop people chatting when the time is up.

(3) *Parenting and Parenting Plus*. First we ask participants to think about what being a parent involves and to call out the ideas which occur to them. They are not intended to think long and hard about it, but to let us have their immediate reactions. As many readers will know this is called 'brainstorming'. It is helpful for one leader to stand in the middle of the group to relay ideas to the second leader, who can then note them down on paper pinned to the wall or on a flip chart for those who are sophisticated enough to have one. Once people get

started, comments usually flow thick and fast. We finish up with a list of words like love, patience, responsibility, hard work, play, fun, frustration, worry, and many more in a similar vein. When this list is exhausted we ask participants to think about the kind of 'extras' which might be involved in being foster or adoptive parents and to go through the same brainstorming routine. These ideas are written up on a separate sheet of paper so that we can compare the two. In this way participants themselves identify some of the extra tasks which they will be undertaking and jointly establish some significant differences, including the existence of biological parents, dealing with a child's separate history, insecurity, lack of trust, confusion and so on.

(4) *How will it affect our family?* Participants are divided into two small working groups and given worksheets entitled 'How's our family going to react?' These sheets include quotations from members of the extended family and neighbours of people who are caring for special needs children. Some quotations are favourable and others resentful. We ask participants to consider these comments in relation to their own families and to anticipate how they will cope with such reactions. The groups are given sheets of paper so that they can record their deliberations, and we ask that a spokesman is delegated to report back when the two groups come together to discuss their ideas. This exercise can be used to emphasise the importance of talking about plans to foster or adopt with family and friends, sharing some of the likely problems with them, and thinking about how to deal with possible hostility or withdrawal of support. We have not tried to introduce role play here, although it might be useful if participants (and leaders) feel sufficiently relaxed and confident.

(5) *Challenges and rewards.* To finish off the first session we show the very informative film, 'Where the Love Starts'. This includes information about children in care and features young adults who have grown up both in children's homes and with adoptive families, and foster and adoptive parents, talking about their experiences – good and bad. The film has considerable emotional impact so we ask group members to remember something which particularly strikes them, and which we will use to start off the next session.

Session Two: being in care

(1) *Introduction.* The group leader summarises significant points

from the last session and explains that during this meeting we will try to grasp how children feel about being in care. Participants contribute what they remember from the film, which might be the foster mother who spent many nights looking for a runaway teenager, the prospective adopters who were driven to distraction, and nearly defeat, by the insecure and demanding behaviour of the little boy who joined them, or the adopted adult who talked about her need to know more about her biological parents. This reinforces the film's impact and helps to consolidate what people have learned.

(2) *Reasons for coming into care.* Participants are asked to 'brainstorm' why children may come into care, and their comments are recorded as previously explained. In this way people come to appreciate the wide range of reasons for admission to care, and to understand the interaction of various factors which may lead to distortion of relationships or family breakdown. Following participants' own observations, we compare what they have said with statistical information. This presents the reality of a high proportion of temporary admissions due to parental hospitalisation, and makes it clear that we are *not* talking about orphans, but about children who have existing biological parents and experiences which they will want to remember, talk about, and have accepted by foster or adoptive parents.

(3) *Separation and loss.* We are lucky here to have a superb tape-recording made by a young adult whom I shall call Joan. After numerous admissions to care she and her half-brother were placed in a children's home, following the death of their mother. At this time Joan was six years old and her brother a little younger. They remained in residential care until they were placed with the same foster parents when Joan was fourteen. On this part of the tape Joan refers to how little she remembers about her mother and her life prior to the children's home. She comments sadly that she has no photographs of her mother and cannot remember what she looked like. Participants appreciate the enormity of Joan's loss and recognise that, while they can restore memories or gaps in information by recourse to their extended families, Joan has no way of filling this void.

(4) *Being received into care.* Participants are divided into two small workgroups and given sheets which record children's remarks about how they felt when they were admitted to care. One group is asked to consider how these quotations make them feel and the other to discuss

how the children feel. Each group is again given a sheet of paper and a spokesman asked to report back. The exercise helps people to identify and express some strong reactions and to understand how coming into care feels for children in this situation. It prepares them for their likely responses to the 'real thing' and encourages an appreciation of how the world looks from a child's point of view.

(5) *Falling apart.* Joan talks on tape about how she felt when she was told at fourteen years old, that her brother had a different biological father. She recalls her reactions vividly, saying that she felt as though she had lost part of herself, that she was nothing, that her world had fallen apart. Joan then goes on to discuss the lack of continuity in any relationships while she was in care – social workers did not talk to her about the future. Residential and field social workers came, and then disappeared. Group members often express feelings of outrage that Joan was not told about her brother earlier and that 'the system' apparently let her down so badly. We are able to use Joan's comments to illustrate how a factual change in biological relatedness had such a severe impact, because it denied something which she had always taken for granted and removed the last vestige of security from her uncertain world and vulnerable sense of identity. This tape also emphasises the importance of continuous and dependable relationships, and the significance of parenting in this context.

(6) *How would you feel?* Now comes the tough part! Because we think that understanding loss is vitally important for foster and adoptive parents, we ask the participants to close their eyes for a few seconds and to remember their feelings on experiencing some kind of loss, separation or new and daunting situation. They are then asked to 'brainstorm' their responses which are written up in the usual way. There is little hesitation in producing a list which includes feelings of anger, confusion, despair, loneliness, fear, anxiety, pain, and so on. The list is used to illustrate two major points. First, that participants are able to understand how children will feel on coming into care or moving into a new family, and therefore have the emotional resources to help them. Secondly, that in coping with children who are reacting to loss, their own feelings and memories may come to the fore and give them a sharp slap in the face. They will need to be aware of this possibility and be ready to distinguish between their own feelings and those of children in their care.

(7) *Living in a children's home.* Joan provides a breathing space after the last few minutes by talking about the characteristics of residential

care. She refers to well-intentioned, but as she perceives them, condescending visitors; structured and inflexible routine; lack of privacy and personal belongings. This promotes group discussion about the differences between children's homes and family life. While recognising that families also have routines and members do not have unlimited privacy, ways can be explored of introducing flexibility and accommodating some of the needs of children who join new families from residential care.

(8) *Trying to understand being in care.* Participants are divided, into their two work groups and given sheets which record children's reactions to being in care. One group is asked to consider how it feels to be in care and the other to discuss what effect it may have on children. The procedure is as previously explained, with the full group coming together to pool ideas.

Session Three: the child's family

(1) *Introduction.* As usual a summary of what we have covered so far and an opportunity for group members to ask any questions arising from the last session. A leader reminds the group that the child's family and background have already been identified as important areas, and that this session will concentrate on looking at related issues in detail.

(2) *Feelings about biological parents.* Group members had previously been given a hand-out to read before this session concerning a foster mother's attempts to help her foster child unravel a complicated and unhappy history. The hand-out chronicles this process including contact between the child and her mother and father, the mother's subsequent failure to keep promises or maintain contact, the discovery that the man she thought to be her father was in fact her stepfather, and so on. Two small work groups are convened, and one asked to think about the literature from the child's point of view and the other to put itself in the position of the foster parents. Recording and reporting back to the full group is arranged as usual. This exercise familiarises participants with the fact that children have significant, complicated, and sometimes unhappy biographies which must be accommodated by their foster or adoptive families. It helps people to anticipate their own and a child's feelings about this and to begin to work out how they will deal with anxieties about helping children to understand the past. Discussion also highlights the

constructive elements of this work by demonstrating the importance of foster and adoptive parents' support and understanding during this process, and the beneficial outcome for children who are able to grasp the good and bad parts of their experiences and of their biological parents.

(3) *Reactions to biological parents.* The 'Parenting Plus' worksheet is used for this section. It contains quotations from foster parents about sometimes distressing and hostile behaviour from biological parents, and instances where the latter have shown apparent disregard for their children's welfare. The whole group is asked to read this sheet, following which we discuss reactions. This exercise has several advantages. First, participants are likely to express anger about biological parents. We can then let them know that this is not surprising or unacceptable – they *are* going to feel angry when children are disappointed or their task as foster or prospective adoptive parents is made so difficult. Secondly, having established this point, discussion can then move on to distinguish between their anger and how they are able to help children cope with these problems and understand what is happening. Participants recognise that they are responsible, with social work support, for dealing with their own reactions, that if they do not handle these appropriately tensions will develop in family relationships, and that this transmission of anger or hostility is likely to result in conflict and confusion for children in their care. Thirdly, the quotations enable the group to consider why biological parents behave in this way, and to identify the mixed emotions which are felt when their children are being given care, support, and positive experiences which they are unable to provide.

(4) *Handling the child's background.* Participants are asked to consider how they know, or find out about their past, and to 'brainstorm' their ideas. A list is completed as usual which includes references to photographs, documents, family mementos, important family occasions such as weddings and funerals, access to grandparents and members of the extended family, and so on. It readily becomes apparent that for children who have been in care for a long period, such aids to memory are not always available. A group leader then goes on to explain about the compilation of 'life story books'. Books are worked on with children and will include any material which records and helps them to understand the past. A 'typical' book might contain some written explanations, photographs of significant people and places, maps, a family tree, a cherished birthday card, the child's

own drawings and so on. Once again group discussion draws out several points. It is sometimes helpful for foster or adoptive parents to be involved in working on these books; if children see that they are able to accept the past, sharing and talking about it may become less difficult. Foster and adoptive parents need help in coping with some mixed feelings about this; prospective adopters, particularly, may find it hard to come face to face with a child's past and significant others and to have this presented in such a concrete and immediately available way. Thought must be given to ways of communicating painful information to children. Group members spend some time discussing this topic and are able to express anxieties about harming children and damaging relationships through such disclosures.

(5) *Leaving the children's home*. Here Joan talks on tape about her expectations of family life before she was placed with foster parents. Reference is made to freedom, discos, possessions, and so on. Participants are able to consider how the reality of family life matches up to these expectations and to discuss how they will handle roles, discipline, setting boundaries and limiting demands.

(6) *Moving in*. Group members divide into their work groups. One has the task of considering what they take for granted about family life, and the other is asked to discuss how they can make children feel accepted and 'at home' on moving in. Ideas are listed, reported back and discussed in the full group. This helps participants to be more self-conscious about taken-for-granted routines, attitudes and values and to appreciate that some of these may be alien to children who are joining them. It illustrates that some things, for example honesty and being able to leave money around, are so taken for granted that they are not explicitly recognised. Participants are able to anticipate changes, potential difficulties, conflict of values, and adjustments which they will have to make.

(7) *Arriving*. Joan recalls her fears and mixed feelings during the first few days of placement with foster parents. She talks about her inability to cope with choices, new experiences, and relative independence. Group discussions develop an awareness of children's feelings and reactions at this time.

Session Four: living with a family

(1) *Introduction*. Summary of areas covered so far and an opportun-

ity to raise questions about material from the last session. A leader reminds the group that we have now reached the point where children move into placement and have given some thought to how they feel about this transition. The present session aims to consider developing relationships and coping with some difficult behaviour.

(2) *Initial worries*. In order to link up with the end of the last session, Joan's tape is played and she continues to talk about coping with new experiences. Here, Joan refers to her fear of meeting new people and her lack of confidence in conversation and making relationships. She recalls how her social incompetence irritated her foster parents. Once again, this focuses the group's attention on how children feel about new and alien experiences, and helps participants to be aware of a potential gap between their expectations and children's needs and abilities.

(3) *Learning confidence*. More of Joan talking about how she gradually learned to cope with family life and developed confidence in a number of areas. Despite making progress in settling in, however, she graphically describes her continuing fear of 'being sent back' to the children's home. We are able to link Joan's fears with much of the group's previous discussion about insecurity and lack of trust and to anticipate how participants will cope with testing behaviour.

(4) *Placement creates new relationships*. Here we use some 'Parenting Plus' material to demonstrate that children do not just slot into families, while relationships remain the same. When a child arrives the whole balance of existing relationships, patterns of interaction and networks of communication are likely to change. The material consists of a cartoon drawing of a husband and wife having a fierce argument about what to do with their foster daughter who has apparently stolen a watch and lied about it into the bargain. Participants divide into their work groups. One group is asked to play out the conversation, to develop it if possible, and to consider what the foster parents are feeling, and the other group is asked to discuss the incident from the foster child's point of view. Reporting back and full discussion takes place as usual. This is an excellent exercise. It emphasises the degree of strain and conflict which might occur between foster parents who must recognise their own needs and expectations; highlights participants' own values about stealing and lying; and provides a concrete opportunity to work out how they would handle such a situation. There is usually much lively discussion, and on occasions the group leader has been required to

mediate in some heated arguments. Using the two work groups in this way encourages a dialogue between the 'child's group' and the 'foster parents' group' and illustrates their different perceptions, feelings, fears, and difficulties which may arise through confrontation and poor communication.

(5) *Family pressures*. Thus far the group has considered the advantages of family placement. In this section we use Joan's tape to identify some of the tensions which may arise when children move from residential care to the emotional closeness of family life. Joan talks about coping with her foster parents being angry, miserable, ill, occasionally 'tipsy', and having rows. She points out that residential care staff had different moods but that any emotional impact felt by the children was muted by expectations of professional conduct, physical space, and the sheer number of children. This emphasises again that facets of family interaction, which are taken for granted by participants, will have additional significance and may pose problems for children in their care.

(6) *Challenges and rewards*. Work groups are convened, one to list challenges and the other to identify rewards. Comparison of the two lists shows much overlapping. As well as serving to make both challenges and rewards explicit, this exercise again encourages participants to look at their own needs and expectations and to measure these against the tasks which have been discussed throughout group meetings.

(7) *Parenting needs*. We come back to Joan's tape here. By now the group is very much involved in Joan's story and sympathetic to her feelings. She remembers that the placement disrupted, and that although she and her brother tried to please their foster parents, this was accepted as the way any child would be expected to behave in a family. Thus, Joan concludes, they grew to love their foster parents but were unable to demonstrate this in a sufficiently obvious way. In answer to the interviewer's question about what Joan thought her foster parents wanted, she replys 'to love them, I suppose'. This section of tape really brings home the possibly unrecognised demands and expectations of Joan's foster parents, and their inability to see the world through Joan's eyes.

(8) *Conclusion*. We are aware that in leaving the group with Joan's foster home breakdown there is a danger of totally demoralising participants. They are therefore encouraged to remember the benefits

which Joan herself identified in the placement and to consider her explanation for the disruption. The group is able to see that foster and adoptive parents must try to sort out their own needs and that their expectations of a child must be geared to the child's experiences and perceptions, not to those of the adult and rational world.

Application forms are distributed and explained, and we ask participants to give careful thought to what they have learned during group discussions before letting us have their completed forms back. There is time for further questions before the group disperses.

Group meetings: comments

I know of no better way to help prospective foster and adoptive parents begin the process of self-assessment than through the use of group discussion. Several points should be noted about this approach. First, the value of group meetings is not that social workers can talk to several people at once, and thus do the job more quickly. The structure and content of meetings are designed to help participants learn about the needs of children and to work out, for themselves, what they are able and willing to do.

Secondly, the function of group leaders is therefore not to make long speeches but to hold the different strands together, facilitate discussion by prompting, mediating, clarifying and enabling participants to express different points of view. Group leaders are responsible for helping people to feel comfortable and must therefore be well prepared, ensure that practical arrangements run smoothly, explain exercises clearly, and be aware of the responses and mood of participants. They must remember to avoid letting people feel overwhelmed by potential difficulties and to convey an attitude of confidence, enthusiasm and humour. Leaders should be alert to the possibility that some exercises may engender painful feelings or memories for participants and that in subsequent discussion individuals may need a breathing space. If anyone shows signs of distress they should be approached in a quiet moment so that they may be reassured, given the opportunity for further discussion, and allowed to see that the leader is sympathetic and understands their reactions.

Thirdly, the NFCA 'Parenting Plus' sessions are based on very good learning material, but provided that social workers know what they want to achieve, it is possible to design and produce their own course content with little difficulty. It should be remembered, however, that any course must have variety, must allow for physical movement of participants, and must use material which is relevant and manageable. In the course outlined above, we use a range of materials and techniques including a film, tape, work sheets, exercises, small work groups reporting back, full group discussions, 'brainstorming' and participants own experiences. It is best for leaders to withdraw while the small work groups are in action, so that members feel free to get on with the task and say what they think and feel. Our approach is not to say, 'Here is a problem, see if you can come up with the right solution and we will judge your answers', but 'Have a look at this situation, let us know what you think and feel about it, and try to sort out the pros and cons of different ways to tackle it.'

Fourthly, throughout the sessions participants repeatedly come back to the vital distinction between their adult way of viewing and controlling their world, and a child's inability to think, communicate, analyse, and deal with feelings and experiences in the same fashion. Group members appreciate that they have the capacity to see the world as it appears to a youngster, but that in order to do this they must stop in their tracks, think about the child's background, and be willing to suspend some of the things which they take for granted.

Fifthly, training courses for group leaders who will use the NFCA 'Parenting Plus' material include foster parents as well as social workers because, it is argued, foster parents should act as co-leaders in subsequent discussion groups. Experienced foster or adoptive parents may either help to lead sessions or be included as participants. Sixthly, material distributed during group meetings may usefully be supplemented by further exercises and write-ups for families to tackle at home. The form and content of the particular sessions which I have described do not, for example, include any attention to the law. Legal details become more relevant and understandable in relation to a particular placement. However, a written account of the main elements of law relating to children is provided for background information and future reference, together with reading lists, useful addresses and other relevant material.

Group meetings: babies and toddlers

Separate sessions are held for couples who are very clear that they wish to adopt babies or very young children. These are not arranged before individual work begins, but at some point during the course of personal interviews. We consider it appropriate to distinguish between 'special needs groups' and 'baby groups' in this way because of the exploratory nature of the former and the different needs and perceptions of group members. The advantages of group discussion and the approach already noted are evident in both situations. However, we consider that it is possible to deal with the material for couples wishing to adopt babies and toddlers in three sessions rather than four. Content is organised as follows:

Session One: setting the scene

(1) *Introduction.* This largely takes the form of introductory comments made to members of the 'special needs group' but with appropriate modifications, given the focus on adoption and the age range of children being considered. However, emphasis is again placed on helping participants to feel comfortable, to use group meetings in the way which is most helpful for them, and providing an opportunity for discussing issues and ideas.

(2) *Introducing ourselves.* This exercise is carried out in the same way as for the 'special needs' group.

(3) *Parenting and Parenting Plus.* Again this exercise is carried out in the same way as for the 'special needs' group. It helps participants to establish, for themselves, the additional tasks which they will face as adoptive parents. These will involve recognising that their child was born to different parents, explaining adoption and reasons for placement, and talking about biological parents. 'Brainstorming' and subsequent discussion aims to achieve what Kirk has termed 'acknowledgement of difference'. (See Chapter 7 for reservations to this general point.)

(4) *How will it affect our family?* A modified list of quotations from neighbours, friends and extended family is provided, and two work groups are convened to consider these in relation to their own circumstances. Reporting back and full group discussion occurs in the usual way. This exercise facilitates discussion not only of attitudes to adoption, but of how some couples have coped with childlessness, managed information about their condition, and dealt with social conflicts and tensions generated by their significant others.

(5) *Choosing adoption.* This allows for discussion in the full group about the process through which participants have chosen adoption as an acceptable alternative to biological parenthood. It enables members to explore the implications of parenthood through adoption

from their own and a child's point of view, and to consider changing social attitudes towards related factors – for example illegitimacy, parental rights, early placement of babies with developmental queries or risk factors, matching, and so on.

Session Two: talking about adoption and biological parents

(1) *Introduction.* A brief summary of significant points from the first session and an opportunity for participants to raise questions. A group leader reminds members that we have already identified some 'pluses' in relation to adoptive parenthood and that this session will aim to consider the importance of talking about adoption and biological parents.

(2) *Biological parents.* Although the issue of access to birth records (Section 26, 1975 Children Act) will have been discussed with applicants individually, this is explained again and group members are encouraged to explore their reactions. A leader will tell participants about research into the operation of this Section, reinforcing both adoptees' loyalty towards their adoptive parents and their need to have extensive background information. Following full group discussion, two work groups are convened and given a list of quotations from parents who are thinking about placing their children for adoption. One group is asked to 'think itself into' the situation and feelings of these parents, and the other to consider participants' reactions as prospective adopters. Reporting back and full group discussion takes place as usual. This exercise aims to help group members develop a sympathetic awareness of the perceptions and feelings of biological parents. The two work groups are often able to continue a dialogue between the 'biological parents' group' and the 'adoptive parents' group', thus thrashing out any areas of tension, uncertainty and competing needs.

(3) *Handling the child's background.* As in the 'special needs group', participants are asked to 'brainstorm' how they know or find out about the past. A similar list is produced and group members are able to identify the importance which they attach to having access to this information. They can then move on to accepting that adopted children are likely to feel confused and 'cut off' from the past if they are not given access to knowledge about themselves and their biological families.

(4) *Talking about background.* At the end of the last session, participants were given a write-up covering information about biological parents and reasons for placement, and were asked to familiarise themselves with this material for the present meeting. The write-up refers to an imaginary situation, but includes some problematic information, for example, conception as a result of a casual relationship, the mother's initial wish for an abortion and subsequent negative feelings about the pregnancy, the father's anti-social and violent behaviour, and so on. Small work groups are convened and asked to construct the equivalent of a life story book, with space for photographs where they consider their inclusion appropriate. Doubts, difficulties and worries are discussed in the full group. This exercise helps participants to come to grips with ways of making information directly accessible to adopted children and, importantly, to work out how to convey such information in a constructive and sympathetic form. It also identifies any ambivalent feelings about biological parents, allows prospective adopters to acknowledge these, and encourages them to evaluate their own needs in relation to those of children who may be placed with them.

Session Three: placement

(1) *Introduction.* Summary of points covered so far and discussion of any questions which have arisen from previous sessions.

(2) *How does it happen?* A group leader presents information about attitudes to matching children and prospective adopters, the pros and cons of direct placements from hospital versus a period of pre-adoption fostering, medical examinations of babies and young children who are placed for adoption, meeting biological parents, and feelings of prospective adopters. These topics are considered by the full group and usually generate active discussion and exchange of views. Although there will be individual consideration of these areas during interviews, this pooling of ideas may influence attitudes and enable prospective adopters to look at alternative approaches.

(3) *Support services.* At this point we introduce a health visitor to the group who discusses her role, the availability of support services, and provides guidance about health and developmental needs of babies and young children. Prospective adopters have many questions to ask about the service provided by health visitors and about matters concerning child care.

(4) *Conclusion.* A group leader sums up discussion over the past three sessions and answers any outstanding questions. A framework is outlined for completing the procedure and subsequent events.

It should be appreciated that many of the comments made earlier about the form, content, and purpose of group sessions, apply equally to 'special needs' and 'baby' groups.

Social workers and applicants: interviews

I have already outlined the basic approach which should obtain when social workers and applicants begin working together. The Working Party on Fostering Practice (1976) and the Advisory Council on Child Care (1970) detail information to be collected and topics to be discussed during work on fostering and adoption applications, respectively. Many agencies now use Form F, devised by British Agencies for Adoption and Fostering, as the standard tool for working both with those who wish to adopt babies and those who plan to foster or adopt children with special needs. If applicants have attended group discussions before moving on to individual interviews, it is worth giving some thought to whether the same worker should be involved in both parts of the procedure. Although there is little guidance on this matter, Dillow (1968) points out that couples attending group meetings held by her agency tended to perceive help, preparation and support as coming from the group rather than from social work leaders. When applicants and social workers subsequently met at interviews it appeared that the former were 'shy and awkward' and found it difficult to develop relationships on this basis. So significant was this problem that social workers who had acted as group leaders did not continue working with couples during the next stage.

Form F consists of main topic headings with detailed sub-questions and a space for recording information and observations. Because it is designed in this way, important areas are immediately accessible and questions are sufficiently sub-divided to enable applicants to discuss them and to attempt a written answer. Topics to be covered are as follows:

(1) *Individual profiles of male and female applicants.* This includes a 'pen picture' of each applicant describing physical appearance, colouring, and impression of temperament; a description of family background, experiences of growing up, past and present family relationships, lifestyles of extended family members; type of education and attitude to own experience of school and learning; occupa-

tion and feelings about work satisfaction, future plans, likely job changes; interests and leisure time and how far activities are jointly pursued; personality and philosophy of life, including attitude to religion, flexibility towards others' beliefs, approaches to problems – in other words the values, aspirations, and personal qualities which people bring to bear upon planning and making sense of their lives.

(2) *Marital history and present relationship for both applicants.* This requires brief details of courtship and marriage and encourages discussion about coping with problems, communication between partners, areas of strain, ways of dealing with disagreements and anger, feelings about mutual support and understanding, whether and how tenderness and concern are expressed, in what areas one partner may be dominant, how roles and expectations are worked out. Some couples may have become more conscious of these areas as a result of previous breakdown in relationships or shared stresses, for example, bereavement, redundancy, financial problems, illness, pressure from extended family, and so on. Others may not have considered such questions in any depth. Helping couples to look at these aspects of interaction facilitates a developing awareness of how fostering or adoption will influence their relationship and the ways in which they may cope with some associated strains and conflicts. Illustrations may be used to focus discussion; I often refer to the quite common behaviour of older children who initially relate to only one partner, or may actively work to disrupt existing family relationships. The relatively sudden arrival of a baby will require emotional readjustments and will impose a variety of pressures on role allocation, communication, and previously taken for granted patterns of interaction. Giving conscious consideration to present relationships will enable couples to anticipate the impact of fostering or adoption, and to take into account their willingness and ability to cope with this.

(3) *Childlessness/Attitudes to further children.* Information is recorded about reasons for childlessness, and discussion encouraged about how couples have coped with any inability to have their own children, how far they have accepted adoption as a desirable alternative, what kinds of anxieties and expectations they have about adoption, awareness that painful feelings may be revived, for example, when talking to their adopted children about origins and biological parents.

(4) *Parenting capacity of both applicants.* This section considers how applicants view their role as parents. Some focus is provided by

exploring applicants' perceptions of their own parents and ways in which they might want to do things differently, relationships with their own or other people's children, any difficulties in dealing with parental responsibilities, expectations of parenthood. Discussion of this topic will involve ideas about children's needs and how these are to be met, accepting children's individuality, dealing with challenges to parents' values and adolescent rebellion, coping with children's growing independence and attitudes towards sexual development and relationships. If applicants are considering caring for children with special needs, examples or additional information may be introduced to help them anticipate particular challenges and ways in which they may respond to these.

(5) *Pen pictures of each child in the household.* Applicants are asked to think about children who are already living with them, in terms of physical characteristics, personality, intelligence, special needs, interests, feelings about fostering or adoption plans, particularly significant relationships with other siblings or either parent. Decisions about temporary or permanent placements and the needs of children who will be joining new families, necessitates full discussion of family structure and existing relationships between all members.

(6) *Extended family.* This refers to important relationships with the wider family and neighbourhood, frequency and quality of contact with others, and availability of support networks. The significance of other people's reactions to placement may vary depending on whether a child is placed on a temporary or permanent basis. Hostility must be anticipated and applicants encouraged to think about how they will deal with this. It is not uncommon for worried friends and relatives to suggest that a child should be 'sent back' if they see applicants becoming worn down by difficult and rejecting behaviour. Some social workers find it helpful to work out an 'ecomap' with prospective foster and adoptive families, which illustrates important links with resources and areas of activity, the direction of resource flow, and the strength of relationships between different sectors of the map. This not only helps the social worker to get the lines and significance of interaction clear, but illustrates this diagrammatically for applicants who play a central part in drawing out the map. Writing about this approach Hartman suggests that,

an ecological view not only recognises that stress and conflict are always a part of the world of any living system, but also that some sort of balance must be achieved between stress and support, between demands and resources, for a system to survive and grow. The ecomap leads a family to assess whether they have an excess of resources, whether they are already stressed, or without sufficient support.   (Hartman, 1979, p. 34)

(7) *Family life style*. Applicants are encouraged to think about how their family operates, what kind of value system guides decision-making and interaction, how is time spent, what things are considered to be important. The sub-questions on Form F refer to whether family members are open or controlled in expressing their feelings; whether activities are carried out together or individually, what links there may be with groups/clubs; attitudes to money, food, health and ill-health; the importance of school achievement; what kinds of rules exist, how strict they are and how infringement and misbehaviour are punished, who is responsible for discipline, how special occasions are celebrated, what special roles are defined, the nature of expectations about how a child will fit into or alter family patterns. Full discussion of these areas really helps a family to look at the likely impact of placement and helps social workers when they are considering children for long-term or permanent integration into a family.

These questions also enable some exploration of how applicants will be able to respond to a particular child's needs. If, for example, family members are very open in expressing feelings and see themselves as 'cuddlers', how will they deal with a frightened, withdrawn child who associates touch with abuse, sexual interference, or pain? A quiet, uncertain child may be overlooked or cause tension in a family which thrives on noise and activity. If mealtimes are viewed as a family institution and an important social occasion for members, how will they respond to a child whose anxieties are displayed by overeating, being sick, refusing to eat, persistently coming in late for meals? A concern with school achievement and homework must be assessed in relation to a child who might act out problems at school, refuse to go, forget to bring back homework, or avoid doing it. Forms of punishment should be considered with regard to a child's previous experience where smacking and being confined to a bedroom may carry different associations and levels of fear or anxiety. Working on this section can be beneficial in helping families to sort out basic values, expectations, and patterns of interaction, in a way which clarifies their willingness and ability to cope with different kinds of children and placements.

(8) *Motivation and present understanding of adoption/fostering tasks.* This section is designed to explore applicants' needs and expectations, and the appropriateness of temporary or permanent placements. Experiences which may be relevant to applicants' feelings such as childlessness, bereavement, separation are also discussed in relation to the rewards which they may anticipate from fostering or adopting. While considering types of placement, related factors will also be given attention, for example, feelings about contested adoption applications, toleration of fostering prior to adoption and the purpose of introductions to children where appropriate.

(9) *Contact with natural family and people from the child's past.* Although the degree of parental contact is likely to differ between temporary and permanent placements, recognising the importance of a child's past and significant others, and dealing with painful memories, comprise vital tasks for foster and adoptive parents. Discussion of this topic covers expectations of contact with the child's parents and relatives, ways of maintaining a child's links with the past, helping a child to understand what has happened. Applicants who are thinking about offering temporary placements will need to consider their attitudes towards biological parents and ability to work sympathetically with them, co-operating with social workers in plans for rehabilitation, coping with a child's confusion and distress, understanding parents' reactions, and ways of helping parents to gain confidence, develop knowledge of child care and parenting skills, and improve the quality of interaction with their children. Applicants must be encouraged to express any doubts or anxieties and time must be spent preparing them to cope with difficult situations. Many applicants will want to talk over how they should handle painful information about a child's past, while maintaining a balance between honesty and presenting the strengths and weaknesses of biological parents in an acceptable way. Fears about harming or upsetting children by talking about the past will also be explored.

(10) *Expectations of the child's background.* This enables applicants to consider their feelings about heredity and such factors as illegitimacy, deviant behaviour, law breaking, family violence, alcoholism, mental illness, retardation, and so on, which might occur in a child's biological family. There is an opportunity to talk about special tasks, for example, where couples are anticipating transracial placements and the need to cope with children's possible confusion, hurtful remarks, racial identity and wish for information about their cultural background. Social workers must help applicants to be realistic about

their fears and prejudices and to be honest about their ability to accept that no child will present a 'carbon copy' of themselves.

(11) *Expectations of child to be placed.* Applicants will talk about the hopes and ideas which they have about children who may be placed with them. This is particularly relevant for those undertaking long-term and permanent placements, but it is also important to maximise success in temporary placements by choosing foster parents who can cope with the tasks associated with particular children. Discussion concerns understanding difficult behaviour and working out appropriate responses. Reference should be made to delayed or excessive affection, testing, acting out, withdrawal, attention-seeking, rivalry, bed-wetting, stealing, and so on. Social workers should explore whether there is any behaviour which would be intolerable to applicants, and to assess willingness and ability to deal with special needs, for instance, physical or mental handicap, particular educational requirements, debilitating illness, among others. While applicants may find it problematic to consider these characteristics in isolation from knowledge about a particular child, it is possible to determine a framework within which realistic linking may be given further discussion or speedy temporary placements may be appropriately effected.

(12) *Accommodation and neighbourhood.* This section provides factual information about accommodation, playspace, number and type of family pets, local amenities, racial mix, access to particular resources, transport and practical household arrangements.

(13) *Social worker's assessment.* Social workers are asked for an assessment (made jointly with applicants) of the kinds of children and placements with which families could most successfully cope, including any special skills or qualities which they have to offer. Form F notes that if there is any disagreement between social workers and applicants, 'it is important to record this so that they may be considered for the widest possible range of individual children'.

Some concluding remarks

I have already referred to the quality of interaction which should be established when social workers and applicants meet during interviews. Form F, or any other final document, should be a jointly written account. If interviews have been used to explore and discuss issues, then any report should reflect this. It should not be a dogmatic and one-sided assessment of applicants, but should attempt to describe the hard work, struggles, sometimes uncertainties, subtleties, complexities, and pros and cons, which will become apparent when anyone tries to sort out their ideas and feelings about difficult and significant subjects. The final version should include three types of statement which are relevant to most topics covered. These are first, the applicants' views and feelings; secondly, the social worker's observations and evidence accumulated over several interviews; thirdly, a joint interpretation and assessment of information, which guides the use of families as an appropriate resource for particular kinds of children and placements. In accordance with the approach which I have suggested, applicants will be given a copy of the report. This is based on the understanding, made clear at the beginning, that references must remain confidential and will not be included in the copy which applicants receive.

Ways of involving applicants in completing Form F will vary, depending on their confidence, ability, and ease in putting ideas down in writing. Clearly some applicants would not know where to begin if presented with a blank Form F, and it may be more appropriate to suggest that they start off by tackling a single page of fairly basic information, for example, personal profiles. As confidence grows, more complex questions may be introduced. From information provided in this way by applicants, social workers are able to expand discussion, introduce new ways of looking at issues, raise questions and ask for clarification, pose examples, recognise complexities and dilemmas, and encourage family members to explore and work out problems and responses for themselves. This kind of interaction should facilitate a more thorough understanding of tasks related to fostering and adoption, and enable social workers and applicants to develop a secure working relationship which will stand them in good stead later on. Throughout discussion, social workers will extend and consolidate the preparation which applicants experienced during group sessions; reference may often be made to this material and to ideas and feelings expressed during these meetings.

I have not emphasised the importance of a second social worker visiting applicants at some stage during the procedure, because I wonder exactly what is achieved by this exercise. It seems to be common practice that just before 'approval' of an application, another or senior social worker will visit to provide a second opinion. This approach seems to be in line with an assessment/vetting method of operation, rather than the preparation model which I have outlined. However, whatever the approach, it seems that little may be gained from a one-off contact where interaction is likely to be superficial and influenced by all the disadvantages which are associated with assessment and selection. There may be a case for introducing a second social worker but I would consider this to be appropriate for different reasons. It may arise if applicants and a social worker find it difficult to work together, if there is a 'sticking point' over particular views where agreement cannot be reached, or if the applicants request it. Thorough though it may sound, the availability of a second opinion is of little use if the groundwork has not been done and if applicants are approached in such a way as to make impression management their main concern.

Finally, it has to be recognised that applicants and social workers may disagree about ways of tackling problems or the desirability of using families as a resource for particular kinds of children. I have found that this rarely occurs since open evenings and groups enable some applicants to decide that they are unable or unwilling to undertake the tasks involved. However, if an impasse is reached later on social workers should explain their concern as honestly and as clearly as possible. I will return to this topic when considering the role of the adoption Panel.

Although this book is not primarily about fostering, I have referred to foster parents in this chapter because I would argue that the form and content of preparation is appropriate to all those who will be caring for children in whatever capacity this might be.

6
Getting Families and Children Together

'What must I do to tame you?' asked the little prince. 'You must be very patient,' replied the fox. 'First you will sit down at a little distance from me – like that – in the grass. I shall look at you out of the corner of my eye, and you will say nothing. Words are a source of misunderstandings. But you will sit a little closer to me every day.'

Antoine de Saint-Exupery, *The Little Prince*

Linking children and families

So far I have considered working with prospective foster and adoptive parents and preparing children for placement. Now comes the tricky part when we try to get children linked up and placed with their new families. These days the term 'linking' is preferred to 'matching', the latter being associated with an historical situation when there was a realistic choice in the placement of healthy white babies. Current practice emphasises working with prospective adopters towards an understanding and appreciation of each child's individuality. This includes the recognition that a child has been born to other parents and that this may play some part in his or her growing personality and abilities. As in any family, unrealistic expectations of children or excessive parental attempts to mould their children into 'carbon copies' of themselves are likely to engender difficulties for all concerned. Raynor (1980) suggests that 'in recent years much scorn has been heaped on the concept of matching a child to his prospective adopters'. She notes the near impossibility of accurately predicting a baby's future personality, appearance, or intellectual capacity, particularly where there may be virtually no information about one biological parent, and acknowledges that 'there is no question but that some of the matching exercises in the past were carried to absurd lengths'.

However, Raynor's research indicated strongly that 'both adoptive parents and their grown-up children have made it clear that a feeling of likeness is part of the feeling of kinship and that a characteristic of less than happy adoptions is a sense of difference and not belonging'. It is recognised that this sense of likeness may refer to shared values and interests rather than to physical, intellectual, or temperamental characteristics, and may be related to living together rather than to any inherent factors. Nonetheless, Raynor implies that to neglect matching in practice may be unhelpful to adoptive families and children in the long term. Researchers have shown some interest in this area and there is evidence that children who are placed at an early age generally come to resemble their adoptive parents in relation to physical attributes, measured intelligence, hobbies and interests. This is not surprising given a common diet, joint activities, and shared day-to-day conversation. Perceived likeness may certainly be connected to the social processes and exchanges of everyday life but will also depend on relationships which include adopted children as if they had been born to their adoptive parents.

It should be remembered that this experience of belonging and security has been demonstrated to be very important for adoptees and to be indicative of success in adoption outcome. The relationship between characteristics, perceived likeness, a sense of belonging and adoption outcome, is obviously complex and difficult to measure. It must also be associated with the willingness and ability of prospective adopters to accept the validity of socially, rather than biologically defined relationships with their children, to feel and act like 'real' parents, and to establish a balance between their own hopes and expectations and the genetic and personal individuality of their adopted children. Matching in the traditional sense has therefore been eschewed in favour of other considerations, although it is probably still the case that some agencies would avoid a very obvious mis-match, for example, in relation to height or colouring.

Linking babies with prospective adopters should therefore be based on fairly limited criteria such as the religious wishes of biological parents, geography, racial background and any feelings which parents may have expressed when considering adoption for their children. Questions such as 'are prospective adopters prepared to meet biological parents?' or 'will they be able to deal with unpleasant information about conception and background' should not be relevant. If we have adequately prepared prospective adopters and helped them to understand and assess their willingness and ability to handle additional tasks, they should be ready to cope with these eventualities. Identified problems such as physical handicap or Down's Syndrome do, of course, present factors which must be considered in linking babies or very young children with their new parents. Once again preparation and self-assessment of prospective adopters will be important. In some cases we will be dealing with 'risk factors' where the long-term outcome cannot be known. These may include certain physical and mental illnesses or subnormality in biological parents, matters relating to ante-natal care, complications during birth, early non-accidental injury, and so on. Such areas will have been fully explored with prospective adopters who should have considered their own attitudes, values, predjudices and ability to cope with subsequent problems if they should arise.

Although it is difficult to draw up a 'blue-print', discussion with prospective adopters should provide a framework for looking realistically at potential placements. Over the years it seems to have become less and less the case that babies and very young children who need adoptive families do not have some risk factors which must be taken into account. Clearly it would not be sensible to place a child with a high risk of retarded development or subnormality with prospective adopters who anticipate that they would find this difficult to handle. However, I have found that if we spell this picture out when couples first approach an agency and are realistic and honest about the situation, then many prospective adopters are able to shift their focus from the idea of a 'healthy white baby' and to broaden their perspective so that actual or potential complications may be considered in relation to a particular child's needs and characteristics. All of this presupposes adequate preparation, honest discussion between social workers and applicants, realistic self-assessment by the latter, continued support, and making available the fullest possible information about particular children. Such information may include arranging visits to paediatricians and genetic specialists. In any event we must make clear that prospective adopters are working with *uncertainty* and we must be in a position to reassure them about subsequent support, advice, advocacy, and available services if they accept a child who has, or who may develop, significant handicapping conditions.

Linking older children with new families presents us with additional complications. Our completed picture of potential families will include detailed information about their needs and motivation (which plan?), their personalities, the ways in which they cope with stress, interests, values and family lifestyle, experience of difficulties, loss and separation, expectations and hopes for the future, ability to tackle various kinds of behaviour, resiliance and so on.

It is essential that we have similarly detailed information about any child who needs family placement. We must know about the plan for a child's future, perceptions of family life, previous experiences, personality and interests, observed relationships with caretaking adults and children, ways of reacting to and coping with stress, educational needs, family background and characteristics of parents, knowledge and understanding of the past, parents' attitudes towards the plan, assessed reasons for any previous placement disruptions, health and any other 'risk factors' in developmental outcome. Possible linking of older children must be considered along all the dimensions (and often others) which are mentioned above. Knowledge about a child's history and present attitudes, feelings, and behaviour must be extended to include an assessment of likely reactions to family placement. Children who have been rejected and suffered multiple disruptions will all 'test out' their new parents in various ways. The themes are well known and will include reference to 'good' biological parents or previous caretakers, packing bags and threatening to leave, withholding affection and attachment, being disruptive at school, lying, stealing, challenging taken-for-granted values, damaging property, manipulating relationships, bullying children already in the family. Some behaviour may not be directly intended to test out new parents, but may relate to learned responses, coping with particular situations – for example, residential care – and specific patterns of socialisation.

It should be remembered that observed behaviour may change when, for instance, children move from an experience of residential care to that of the expectations, activities and close relationships of family life. I have seen children who are considered to be subdued or 'no trouble' become angry, demanding, or prone to excessive crying as they struggle with the desire to become part of their new family while living with the fear that they are unacceptable and will inevitably be rejected. On the other hand, some children who have bullied their peers, under-achieved at school, and continuously sought attention, may settle down remarkably well with reliable and committed new parents who provide consistent affection, boundaries, and an expectation of security and permanence. However, each child's likely response to placement must be assessed in relation to what is known about previous experiences, present situation, behaviour and personality.

It is helpful to maintain certain ground-rules when considering possible links between children and families. First, some social workers hold the view that people need to try out their motivation and skills by taking a number of short-term placements before they are ready to accept children on a permanent basis. This view may be held particularly strongly in relation to childless couples. I have already argued that short-term fostering and permanent parenting are distinctive tasks and that the choice between these must derive from applicants' assessment of their own needs and motivation. In my view, there is no way in which intentionally temporary placements can prepare couples for the entirely different matter of permanent commitment. There is a world of difference between accepting children and coping with their behaviour as short-term foster parents in the knowledge that they will be returning home, and helping children through months and often years of difficult adjustments as their new and permanent parents. Some social workers also tend to forget that children will react differently in temporary and permanent placements, depending on their expectations and the emotional significance of anticipated events.

Secondly, social workers may also be anxious about placing older and 'damaged' children with childless couples who have no experience of parenting. Once again I will have to differ. Experience of parenting natural-born children provides no guarantee that people will be able to cope with the particular stresses and demands which will be imposed by a newcomer. Older children who need permanent family placement will present more extreme demands and qualitatively different behaviour from children who have grown up in the security of their own families. I have found that many childless couples who have taken on difficult older children have made a strong commitment, have not been in a position where comparisons with own children are often made, and have struggled over long periods to help children deal with their uncertainties and unhappiness. It is also the case that some children cannot cope with the competition, rivalry, and perceived monopoly on family affections which exist when natural-born children have an established position, and prior right of access to their parents. Insecure and demanding children will frequently be destructive towards others and I have heard foster parents say on many occasions that *they* could cope with difficult behaviour if 'it was not for the children'. Knowledge of previous family placement disruptions and a thorough assessment of children's needs, may well indicate that for optimal chances of success there should be no other children already established in a new family.

Thirdly, we will know from discussions with prospective adopters the age range and characteristics of children who might appropriately be placed with them. It is irresponsible for couples who are prepared for and anticipate the placement of a seven-year-old, to be approached about a thirteen-year-old who is already moving towards independence. Given the model of working which I have suggested, I do not believe in making decisions *for* prospective adopters. For example, I would happily talk to a couple who were thinking of a child up to seven years old, about a nine-year-old, if other linking factors indicated the likelihood of a successful placement. What is important here is not only a matter of age but of a child's particular needs, degree of maturity, and capabilities. However, we must listen carefully to the expressed needs of prospective adopters and use this knowledge as a baseline for considering further linking factors.

Fourthly, comes the real nitty gritty. We should have enough information about families and children to make an appropriate link in relation to some fairly complex and subtle areas of personality and lifestyle. Some prospective adopters will be better able to cope with withdrawn children while others will be more confident in setting and maintaining boundaries for those children who 'act out' their unhappiness in socially unacceptable ways. Children who are educationally subnormal will need families which can provide a range of non-academic experiences and avenues for achieving success. Even apparently minor characteristics may be important. For example, I remember a family for whom mealtimes had an important social significance. The whole family came together to exchange news, make plans and to ensure that there was at least one period in the day when they all sat down as a family group. Jane was seven when she joined this family. Her anxieties and unhappiness were expressed in vomiting. When faced with food, particularly in a formal setting, she would avoid eating or eat as little as possible. Quite frequently she was sick. Although Jane was presenting difficulties in other ways, perceived problems became focused around meals, and as often happens, a cycle developed of increasing tension, vomiting and disruption. Family members became angry; Jane became more miserable and her general behaviour deteriorated.

Fifthly, prospective adopters should not be afraid that if they are unhappy about a particular link, we will fail to discuss any further children with them. If an open and honest relationship has been established between couples and social workers, the former should be able to express their doubts and worries. It is vital that they should feel able to say no at an early stage without any apprehension, that if they so do, their names will be 'crossed off the list'. Such a reply should indicate the need for further discussion in order to clarify the possibility of a more acceptable link at a later stage.

Finally, this topic cannot be closed without some reference to linking according to racial and cultural characteristics. Simon and Altstein (1977) have discussed the pressure on public agencies in the United States to abandon transracial adoptions during the early 1970s. Far reaching and organised criticism of this practice has not occurred in the same way in Britain, although efforts have been made increasingly to recruit racially matched families for children. However, the publication of Gill and Jackson's (1983) follow-up study of transracial adoptions, which were arranged by the British Adoption Project during the mid to late 1960s, has prompted greater awareness and criticism of this kind of placement. At the time of this study the adopted children had reached adolescence and in the vast majority of cases the adoptions had worked out very successfully. From their research data Gill and Jackson conclude that 'we can find little support for the criticisms of transracial adoption which are based on the anticipated difficulties for the child'. They did discover that, although the adoptions were successful by conventional criteria of measurement and evaluation, racial background was not perceived by the adolescents or their families as a significant factor in personal identity or group affiliation. The authors note that racial issues may become more important for these adoptees as they move into adulthood. If this occurs, it may be problematic in terms of previous denial or lack of awareness of their race. Gill and Jackson conclude that their study 'has highlighted and underlined some of the fears of the critics of transracial adoption. These black children have been made white in all but skin colour. They have no contact with the black community. Their 'coping' mechanisms are based on denying their racial background' (Gill and Jackson, 1983, p. 137).

For very young children, or those who have spent considerable periods of their lives in care, race and cultural experience may be clearly differentiated. In these cases the choice of transracial adoption placements will remain open. The arguments for and against making this choice are so beset by political and ideological complexities, and sometimes clouded by emotive responses, that I can see little hope of reconciliation. However, what does seem to be clear is that we should continue to recruit families which can provide permanent placements for a whole range of children, including those for whom racial and cultural characteristics are deemed to be significant in linking them with new parents. If the choice boils down to leaving a child without a family placement or transracial adoption, then I would have to opt for the latter. In this case, preparation of prospective adopters *must* include knowledge about, and understanding of, race and culture. Children may be placed transracially but still have opportunities for mixing with peers from the same racial background through school and neighbourhood activities. It is the responsibility of social workers to link children with families where locality, parental values, peer groups, and social attitudes, enhance rather than deny the significance of racial identity in transracial placements.

Introducing children and families

Every so often I stop in my tracks and wonder how on earth we all cope with the enormous responsibility of moving children about and entrusting their future to new families. In some cases, of course, social workers deal with this problem by refusing to take any risks at all. Children may be left in residential care where they are apparently well settled, they may be considered too difficult to place, or social workers may attempt family placement and feel so guilty about subsequent disruption that they give up trying. It is probably during introductions, when decisions must be made and risks inevitably taken, that social workers feel the greatest anxiety. This observation is relevant not only to field social workers but to residential staff who will have seen family placements break down, may well have been left to pick up the pieces, and will now be asked to help children move on to new families. Clearly, the work during introductions must be as thoroughly undertaken as that already carried out with families and children. For the moment I will concentrate on children, other than young babies for whom we will be arranging straightforward adoption placements.

In discussing the work of Barnardo's New Families Project, Kerrane (1979) notes that, initially, agency procedure relied on long introductory periods covering four or five months. Gradually social workers began to reassess this approach because such protracted introductions caused anxiety for everyone concerned and it was recognised that major readjustments cannot be made until children have actually moved in with their new families. The purpose of introductory contact was therefore redefined to reflect more limited and more realistic goals. Kerrane identifies these as first, to allow both family and child to have an initial 'gut reaction' to each other; secondly, to provide an opportunity for sufficient familiarity with people and surroundings for a child to experience some sense of continuity; and thirdly, to help a child separate from previous caretakers and anticipate the future in a new family. In order to achieve these goals it is suggested that the pattern and timing of introductions should be clearly outlined, and understood as comprising a first contact on the child's home territory', a second meeting where the child may be taken out and returned to his or her base, a subsequent visit to the new family's home, an overnight stay for two nights, a longer stay with the family, followed by permanent placement. These arrangements avoid the all too familiar situation where children are packed off to their new families for week-ends over several months. Kerrane's suggested format means that an introductory period should generally not extend beyond three to six weeks, depending on a child's age and other factors.

One of the most important points which is made in Kerrane's discussion is that introductions must be planned, time limited, and directed towards intended placement. This is not self-evident to many social workers who find it difficult to take the responsibility for helping children to make the move into new families. It does not seem to be uncommon for introductions to start on a totally open-ended basis with no plans for assessing progress and no time scale. Children and families are left to get on with it for long periods without an opportunity to talk over their feelings, reactions to each other, anxieties about the future, and so on. In some instances children and families, in effect, make their own decisions or drift into placement during extended stays over school holidays. This represents an unfortunate attempt by some social workers to avoid making decisions, by allowing others to do so for them. It is sometimes argued that they simply do not have the time for arranging satisfactory introductions. As we know, however, such an attitude may well lead to subsequent difficulties and greater anxiety later on if children fail to make the move or placements disrupt. The following steps may offer a useful guide for the period of introductions:

(1) *First meeting*. As suggested by Kerrane this should be arranged on a child's home territory. It should be as informal as possible. This may be achieved by allowing prospective adopters to arrive for tea and to join in with general activities. Some social workers favour 'blind viewings' where a child is not told that visitors have particularly come to meet him or her. Although this arrangement is intended to protect children from disappointment and to remove pressure from prospective adopters, experience indicates that children are rarely ignorant about the purpose of such visits and that if they have been adequately prepared and are given appropriate support, they can cope with a 'false start' to introductions. Unless there are very good reasons for acting differently, I would recommend that we are honest with children and explain that an initial contact may not always lead to continuing introductions if they and the prospective adopters do not feel right about each other.

(2) *Second meeting*. Prospective adopters should again visit the child on home territory, but on this occasion should arrange to go out somewhere where interaction can be relaxed and informal. The child will have the security of knowing that there will be a return to base at the end of the day.

(3) *Third meeting*: The child should be collected, if possible, by the prospective adopters and should spend the day at their home becoming familiar with new surroundings and beginning the difficult process of feeling safe away from present caretakers.

(4) *Fourth meeting*: An overnight or week-end stay with the child's new family. This encourages growing familiarity, increasing security, and an opportunity to become acclimatised to family routine.

(5) *Subsequent meetings*: In my experience older children need longer than one or two week-end visits to feel familiar and safe enough with their new family for a permanent move to be effected. I would normally work to a plan of four week-end visits, moving from one overnight stay to long week-ends from Friday to Sunday evening.

The suggestions above are only intended to present an outline programme. Several other points should be taken into account. For young children up to about five years old, overnight visits are likely to be confusing and to increase a sense of fear and insecurity. When we are introducing children of this age to new parents, it is more appropriate to facilitate intensive contact on home territory and with considerable periods of time spent at the prospective adopters' home. Children may thus become familiar with new people and surroundings but always return to base at the end of the day. It is important for children of all ages to see that present caretakers and new parents are able to accept each other and spend time together. It is also helpful for prospective adopters to prepare their own life story books with information and photographs of their house, pets, extended family and locality. This is useful in so far as it encourages them to explore and look at their family in relation to a child's understanding and perceptions. The book may then be used to ease conversation, enable a child to ask questions, and may be left with a child between contacts.

During the course of introductions it is vital that field and residential social workers, or present foster parents, undertake to carry out specific tasks. Following the first contact, the family's worker must visit in order to help them assess their reactions. After all the analysis and discussion which will have gone on over the past few months, what we want to hear about during this visit is a couple's 'gut reaction'. Despite their concern to achieve a family placement, social workers must be sure not to pre-judge the issue. Discussion must be open-ended and there should be absolutely no pressure on prospective adopters to go ahead if they feel unsure. After the second contact, we have found it helpful to hold a planning meeting which will usually be attended by the family's worker, the child's worker and present caretakers, the prospective adopters, and where appropriate the child. During this meeting we will clarify who is doing what and will organise a programme of future visits. A date will also be arranged for a placement meeting, involving the same people, and to be held a week or so before the end of the programme.

Throughout the introductory period the family's worker should make frequent and regular visits, to discuss the prospective adopter's feelings and any problems which might arise. If such visits are neglected, couples and children may find themselves caught up in introductory contacts despite ambivalent feelings. Occasionally prospective adopters may feel unhappy about a child, but without an opportunity to express and assess their doubts may convince themselves that they need to 'give it a chance', or that they will feel better once they have got to know the child. If prospective adopters feel uneasy about a child but are unable to withdraw from introductions, relationships are virtually guaranteed to get worse rather than better. A couple's ability to express any worries is likely to depend on the kind of interaction which they have had with their worker. However, social workers must be alert to certain questions. When discussing contact with a child what is the quality of prospective adopters' comments? Do they sound enthusiastic, excited, keen on further visits, or do they sound hesitant, restrained, uneasy? Are they looking forward to seeing the child again or are other commitments getting in the way? How do they feel when the child arrives and when a week-end visit has ended? Are they making contact with a child in between visits or is this being avoided? Does their facial expression and physical attitude confirm what they are saying? Are they looking away or finding excuses to talk about other matters? If they have natural-born children, what is the quality of their reaction – are they anxious, demanding, resentful of the proposed newcomer, making attempts to avoid contact? Prospective adopters must be given support to withdraw from introductions at an early stage if their feelings are at all ambivalent.

In my experience uncertainties become evident after one or two contacts, and may readily be identified if social workers make the necessary visits, attend carefully to verbal and non-verbal communication, and are prepared to accept the possibility of discontinuing introductions. It is also important to help new parents set the scene for continuing interaction and final placement. Their immediate reaction, for example, may be to arrange all kinds of outings and to respond to a child's expressed demands. In the long term, however, family life is characterised by some pretty boring and routine activities, some frustration, learning rules and accepting discipline. Despite preparation, being faced with the 'real thing' will bring its own worries and questions and social workers must be readily available to provide help and advice during these early contacts. There may be practical problems; what about meals, bedtimes, spending money, defiance, friends, new routines, family rules, and so on? Or we may be considering more subtle areas of relationships and feelings; how should new parents deal with a child's mixed reactions of excitement, hope, fear and uncertainty, recognition of separation and loss, comparisons with biological parents or present caretakers, clinging or withdrawal, anger at leaving after week-end visits?

While the new family's social worker is proceeding as above, it is equally essential that the child's worker is carrying out a similar task. The field social worker should visit regularly to discuss progress directly with the child if he or she is old enough and to check observations with day-to-day caretakers. In this context residential workers or foster parents have a particularly vital role to play. They will see how children react to going and returning from visits to their new parents and they will be around at bath-times, bedtimes and other occasions when children are likely to express worries or fears about the future. Verbal and non-verbal messages are again important. Caretakers must be alert and make time to pick these up and to allow children a relaxed and safe environment in which half-recognised, and sometimes ill-defined, feelings may be explored. We should be aware of children's reactions to contact. Do they look forward to visits and prepare for them, how do children and prospective adopters greet each other and say good bye, do children talk about their new families between visits and what is the quality of their remarks, do they resist returning to present caretakers, how do they talk about the future, are there changes in mood and behaviour, and so on? Observations should be assessed realistically, bearing in mind children's differing ability to look ahead, remember past events, and to cope with anxiety and uncertainty. Children may present different messages. Not long ago an eleven-year-old boy was being introduced to new parents. He had experienced a foster home disruption and had been in residential care for three years. During every contact and visit to his new parents he saw his future in terms of joining their family, quickly began calling them Mum and Dad, resisted returning to the children's home and asked continually when he could move in. At the children's home he spent his time telling everyone that he was not really bothered about the introduction, could 'take them or leave them', and if he decided he did not like these new parents there were plenty more 'fish in the sea'. He was moody and often in tears. This child's caretakers and his new parents understood his need for a 'cover story' in case anything went wrong and his conflicting feelings of hope and fear. His worker continued preparation by looking at the child's role in making a placement successful and reinforcing the realities of family life, while the caretakers and new parents expressed their awareness of his dilemma and their commitment to helping him move on.

The placement meeting provides an opportunity for everyone to pool their views about the progress of introductions and to make appropriate plans. It is at this stage that those adults who are responsible for a child may begin to resist the final placement. Residential workers who have cared for children from disrupted placements may be particularly worried at this time, and understandably so. I have sat through many such meetings where the 'wobbly knees syndrome' is very much in evidence. Common reservations are that the child and family have not yet had to cope with any significant difficulties, it is such a short period on which to assess future prospects, it is not the right time for a child to change school, the child appears to be moody and unsettled.

In essence, how can we be sure that a child is ready to move, how can we guarantee that new parents will cope, and surely it would be better to defer placement until the child has presented some difficult behaviour and prospective adopters have demonstrated their ability to deal with this. What the adults really mean is that they are afraid of failure and if only the introductions could continue for a little longer they might achieve the reassurance which *they* require. We really must be clear about this. I am convinced that children rarely show significantly difficult behaviour until they are established with their new parents. Initially there will be some problematic areas; children will have to learn about their new parents and expectations of family life, they will explore the boundaries of acceptable behaviour, some may lack social competence, and readjustments must be made by all concerned. However, the most difficult and potentially disruptive elements in relationships will focus on emotional commitment and trust. Prospective adopters will find themselves giving love and reassurance only to be rejected, abused and pushed away. Children will want to accept what is offered only to find that fear and mistrust get in the way. These dilemmas are not likely to be faced, and cannot be resolved, until many weeks and often months into placement. The decision must thus be made on the expressed readiness of children and new parents, their commitment to face the challenges which will inevitably lie ahead, and our observations that the basic steps have been taken to enable the development of a relationship.

There are often clear indicators that children are ready for placement, even in those cases where they cannot say it aloud. They may begin to leave personal possessions with their new parents, there will be changes in the way they talk about the future, moods and attitudes will vary as they move between prospective adopters and present caretakers. I remember going to collect a nine-year-old boy from a week-end visit to his new family and he adamantly refused to come back with me. He rather pre-empted the decision of the placement meeting, arranged for a week later, but he clearly stated his case, settled in with his new family, and is now happily adopted. Children need to understand the framework and timing of the introductory period as well as members of their new family. If they are finding it difficult to grasp arrangements or tolerate delay, it may be helpful to draw a chart where visits to their new parents will be coloured in and important dates, such as the placement meeting, may be indicated. It is necessary for the adults involved to consider children's memory spans, ability to cope with frustration, and perceptions of what is happening. We cannot expect children to return to week-end visits, following a longer stay over school holidays. Neither should we test the growing relationship by setting a child artificial choices. Not long ago it was suggested to me that we should assess the degree of a child's commitment to his new parents by offering him the choice of a visit to them or an evening at the youth club. It is only in the very early stage of an introductory period that mutual reactions are a focus of attention. The purpose of subsequent contact is to facilitate placement, not to increase anxiety and uncertainty by demanding proof of attachment from children or their new parents.

The discussion above has been concerned with the placement of older children and the situation is clearly different for couples who will be adopting babies. However, some of the principles will still apply. Research suggests that even young babies are not 'blank slates'. They express their individuality in a number of ways and therefore prompt different responses from caretakers. We must not assume that every couple and baby will be right for each other, and should not allow prospective adopters to do so either. A similar assessment of feelings and reactions must take place following initial contact between a baby and his proposed new parents. Couples may also need some time to get to know their babies. This can usually be accommodated in the hospital if it is a direct placement, or with the help of pre-adoption foster parents. Feeding, handling, becoming familiar with a baby will increase confidence and ease the baby and new parents into placement.

The placement

An assessment and selection approach to working with new parents implicitly assumes that they have the necessary qualities to be good parents, once their application has been approved. Those who are deemed not to be competent are rejected and those who are considered to be able candidates are accepted. The implication of this model is that 'approved' prospective adopters are somehow inherently qualified to accomplish successfully their parenting tasks and that post-placement support is given relatively little attention. Unfortunately, new parents may pick up this message and think that asking for help signals their failure and incompetence. Placements may founder on mounting anxiety, confusion, tiredness, frustration and sometimes plain panic, because social workers have not been around to identify problems sufficiently early, to provide reassurance about the normality of some difficulties, to help new parents consider alternative tactics, to assist in the analysis of complex situations, and to give continuing strength and support to people who are so engrossed in day-to-day problems that they find it hard to see the light at the end of the tunnel. Whatever the ages of children joining new families, prospective adopters will find themselves facing new dilemmas and making many adjustments. Social workers must build in an expectation of regular and frequent visits, which are designed to help new families and not to criticise new parents.

Although extended family and friends are able to act as a 'sounding board' for discussion of problems, to provide reassurance, and to remind new parents that some behaviour is normal and to be expected from all children as they grow up, their patience and willingness to offer support may inevitably run out. If children are seen to be apparently indifferent, rejecting, or abusive towards their new parents over a long period relatives and friends may begin to question the price which is being paid in terms of family harmony and emotional well-being. I have seen many new parents who feel afraid or unable to talk to members of their usual support networks because they anticipate responses like 'you have done enough for this child, he's wrecking your family, he doesn't want help, he thinks the world owes him a living, you will have a breakdown at this rate, I can't bear to see you in this state . . . it is time you got the social worker to take the child away'. When new parents want to express anger and disappointment, they need to be reassured that this is acceptable, normal, and understandable, not to have their feelings picked up and interpreted as a good reason for terminating the placement. Social workers should have the confidence, knowledge, and experience to respond appropriately when new families are going through a difficult patch, while relatives and friends are likely to depend on personal loyalties and to make immediate and emotional assessments which are not always helpful.

As the placement progresses we must be alert to the importance of arranging contact according to the family's needs. Children will gradually come to depend on their new parents for a sense of security and continuity. Social workers and previous caretakers may well have some feelings of loss and regret as their significance diminishes. New parents will gain in confidence and in their knowledge and understanding of children placed with them, and will want to take responsibility for making decisions, dealing with problems, and acting as parents. As these changes occur social workers must be prepared to stand back and to express their confidence in the ability of new families to function independently. Social work intervention must thus be geared to helping a placement work. Lack of contact cannot be excused because there is not enough time or other things are more important. Too much contact cannot be justified because social workers are over-anxious, feel (probably mistakenly) that they know the child better than anyone else, or are unable to relinquish a child's trust and allow attachment to new parents.

Katz (1979) suggests that the idea of balance or homeostasis is important in our approach to working with new families. Clearly the entry of a child into a family will cause fundamental readjustments in patterns of communication, interaction, and relationships. Our previous knowledge of families and children should enable some assessment of how an existing balance will be upset, and families should be prepared to accept that major disruption is normal and predictable. In attempting to deal with difficulties during placement social workers must therefore view the family as a unit and should not single out the child as a focus of attention, help and change. Similarly if social workers concentrate on the child in placement, other family members may feel isolated, bereft of help, and unable to use the social worker as a source of support and advice. If this happens Katz remarks that,

> they can come to believe that their negative feelings are not normal, to feel guilty over their anger and to develop fears about possible failure of the placement. If they do not see the placing worker as really their worker, they may block communication about these feelings, thereby exacerbating the problems. Thus the worker must open up these areas for sympathetic scrutiny prior to placement.

(Katz, 1979, p. 98)

Working with families requires the kinds of skills which all social workers should be expected to have. Some families may have difficulty in communicating their feelings or worries and may need help and clarification in recognising and expressing these accurately. Complex problems may require a social worker's analytical skills. Observing non-verbal cues, facial expressions, physical attitudes, should enable social workers to identify half-felt anxieties, to encourage people to talk about these, and to establish the kind of atmosphere in which anger and worry do not have to remain hidden or denied. Because social workers are not embroiled in day-to-day conflicts and strong emotions they can provide that degree of stability, continuity, and order, in which it is possible to facilitate discussion and to take a long-term perspective.

One important factor in the long term is the new parents' relationship. When they are tired and spending long hours talking over the difficulties of the day, they can gradually lose touch with each other. Everything becomes centred around a child and his or her feelings and behaviour. This danger sometimes becomes very obvious as was the case when we placed a ten-year-old boy with a childless couple. His mother had chosen to marry a man who was not prepared to take John and this boy had spent two years in care, with no parental contact, before a family was found for him. Apart from the expected problems of soiling, stealing, lying and temper tantrums, John had earnest conversations with his new mother, suggesting that if she divorced her husband, they could spend all their time together. If his new parents attempted to go out together John caused such havoc that initially they did not go, and were eventually left without anyone who was prepared to 'baby sit'.

John could not tolerate any situation where he was excluded from his prospective adopters' company and for weeks on end would creep into their bedroom at night to see what was going on. As might be imagined this couple had little sleep and virtually no sexual relationship. They were trying to combat a growing wedge which was getting between them, tiredness, and communication which seemed to focus inevitably on John and his attempts to oust his prospective adoptive father. Social work help ensured that the new parents understood John's fears, enabled them to express their anger and sheer frustration to their worker rather than yelling at each other, facilitated constructive communication and exchange of feelings between them, provided reassurance that these difficulties would *not* go on forever and gave them the basic strength and optimism to keep going. But one of the most important contributions of their worker was to assert that they must have time together without John, that they should not feel guilty about this, and that John had to learn his new parents could have their own relationship without neglecting their commitment to him as a permanent member of the family. During the time when the couple's support network was inactive, the social worker stayed at home with John while his new parents went out to sustain their relationship. It was a tough and nail-biting slog for everyone concerned, but John did eventually learn that he could trust *both* his new parents and all three members of this family were very happy when the adoption order was made.

Social workers, children, and families should enter into placements with the understanding that much hard work is still to be done. There will be occasions when social workers wonder if this can be achieved or whether a placement should be disrupted. This is always a tough decision. However, there are usually clear indications that a place-ment will not work out and that difficulties are not a normal reflection of expected readjustments and the struggle to reach emotional commitment. It may be that a child presents as continuously depressed, anxious, or withdrawn, or that new parents are constantly irritated by a child and unable to express any feelings of attachment or to recognise any positive characteristics. If a child must be moved then preparation and honest explanation are essential. Sadly, it is not unknown for social workers to move children without telling them what is happening, why they must leave, or where they are going. Following a move we must also pay attention to children's feelings of confusion and loss even if, as adults, we are suffering from a sense of failure and guilt. There is no harm in sharing our disappointment with children and allowing them to be sad and angry. Understanding what went wrong is also important for families, social workers, and children and is something which we cannot afford to neglect. It may be easier to avoid the family and leave a child to the care of others, because we blame the former and are afraid to face the latter. Part of our professional responsibility must be not to opt out of difficult situations, to be aware of our personal feelings and reactions, to learn from and to consolidate experience, and to provide a strong and reliable source of support to others who are hurt. Social workers must, therefore, attempt to identify those factors which influenced disrup-tion and encourage families and children to reach a realistic appraisal of why they were unable to make the necessary readjustments and to develop relationships as a family unit.

Adoption

Having managed the first hurdle of placement, and watched it
develop with a mixture of hope, pride, worry, and sometimes sheer
gratitude to new parents who enable children to become confident
and happy, our next decision concerns the timing of adoption. I have
argued that this plan should be built in from the beginning of
placement and I am convinced that this influences the new parents'
degree of commitment and willingness to hold on to children through
difficult and painful patches. Some social workers would disagree
with me, suggesting that a time scale for adoption puts prospective
adopters and children under pressure. They would prefer to leave the
matter totally open-ended. In my view this is another way of saying
that social workers would prefer to leave decision-making to prospective adopters.

I have several comments to make about this topic. First, part of the
linking process relates to plans for a child's future and the expressed
motivation of prospective adopters to provide a permanent home,
secured by adoption, for any child placed with them. Placing a child
without any time scale for adoption is likely to provoke uncertainty
and anxiety about the agency's willingness to work towards this end
and to provide the necessary backing and support. Building in a
framework for decision making makes it clear that everyone is
working towards adoption, but that there is no pressure to make an
application until the child and family are ready. Secondly, the
framework will depend on a child's age and previous experiences. For
young children (excluding babies) up to about five years old, we may
suggest that adoption is considered about six months into placement.
When placing older children in accordance with the Boarding Out
Regulations we have used the second statutory review, nine months
into placement, as a time when it is appropriate to talk about an
adoption application. Thirdly, throughout our work with prospective
adopters, emphasis will have been placed on the needs and feelings of
children who are joining new families. This must continue to be our
focus. I have seen many children who have suffered multiple moves
and who view adoption as a vitally important seal on their new
parents' commitment and assured security as members of their new
families. These children want and need to be adopted, it represents
the security and normality of belonging to a family where members
share the same name and can plan a common future. Fourthly, it is
unrealistic to put off an adoption application until children have
ceased to show any problematic behaviour. Social workers sometimes
insist that everyone should wait a little longer because children are

still testing out their new parents or because they can foresee problems arising later on. This reflects the same kind of 'wobbly knees syndrome' often seen during introductions. For many of these children adoption is part of the 'treatment' and must be seen as an essential element in a long-term programme aimed at increasing confidence, relationship capabilities, and self-esteem.

For some years now there has been a growing recognition of this point and an acceptance that social work help does not stop when an adoption order is made. The idea of post-adoption support is now commonplace when older children have joined new families. It should be noted, however, that this approach can only be successful if social workers are viewed as helpful and supportive. This perception depends on the quality of relationships which have developed between new parents, social workers and the agency right from the first contact, and reminds us, once again, that a preparation model of working will have long-term benefits for children and families.

In relation to the above points, several illustrations come to mind. Not long ago I received a review report from a senior social worker concerning a nine-year-old girl who had been with her new parents for just over three months. She had been in care for five years and had experienced two foster home disruptions which seemed to be related to her very subtle and manipulative behaviour and her destructiveness towards other children in the foster families. Learning from previous mistakes, we chose new parents who were childless and who were sufficiently intelligent and sympathetic to understand and deal with subtle forms of manipulation. This little girl was beginning to talk about permanency and adoption and I would be prepared to put a large bet on the successful outcome of this placement. However, the senior social worker recommended that adoption was not open for consideration, although the placement was intended to be permanent, because the child was somehow inherently difficult and her new parents would need continuing help. The social worker, however, is neglecting the fact that given an appropriate placement this child is not presenting the same problems as hitherto, that *she* will, I am sure, want to secure her membership of this family through adoption, and that there is no mystical bar to continuing social work help following an adoption order.

Some years ago I was at a review on a twelve-year-old boy who had joined his new family nine months before. He had been in care for seven years and still had many unresolved and angry feelings about his biological mother. The placement had not been easy and his prospective adoptive mother had taken the brunt of this youngster's confusion – he wanted to love her but was afraid to trust her. Every time he came close to emotional commitment, he feared rejection and lashed out physically and verbally. When his anxiety became too great he ran away. The prospective adopters had coped with a great deal but had never wavered in their determination to care for this child. They felt that adoption would demonstrate their commitment, and that although their new son's difficulties would not disappear overnight, he would be better able to cope with them in the knowledge that he was accepted and wanted as a permanent member of the family. The social workers involved were very worried about adoption and throughout the review, which was attended by the child, managed to avoid any direct reference to this possibility. Finally, I asked the youngster if there was anything he wanted to say to us. He drew in his breath, gave a long sigh and said, 'Yes please, when are you going to let me be adopted?' If this child had not been brave (or desperate) enough to utter these words, our own anxieties would have led us to ignore the subject. The unspoken premise that social workers are better able to help a child than new parents who have shared tears, anger, confusion, and given comfort and love on a day-to-day basis is also misplaced. New families will need our help and support but this must be acceptable and derive from mutual trust and respect, not from the exercise of professional control or an assumed monopoly on knowledge and understanding.

Some children are not quite as clear about their wishes as the youngster mentioned above and discussions about adoption must go at their pace. An eleven-year-old had been living with his new family for a year before he began thinking about adoption. He had experienced great difficulty in accepting that he could not return to live with his biological parents and was gradually and hesitantly transferring his emotional attachment to the prospective adopters. Everyone had made it clear to him that adoption was *not* a condition of remaining with his new family, but that this could be achieved if and when he was ready. This youngster made the decision that he wanted to be adopted on at least three separate occasions. Each decision was followed by signs of acute worry, lying, stealing and withdrawing from his new parents. Continued social work help enabled the family to understand what was going on and to approach relationships from the child's perspective. He made his final decision about two years after placement and, in accordance with his wishes, he met his biological mother to say goodbye and visited his recently deceased father's grave. Then, with an almost audible sense of relief he made the emotional commitment to his new family and an adoption order was granted.

I have already discussed social workers' ambivalence about

planning for adoption, and this is no less evident when it comes to decisions about particular children who are already placed with new families. Maintaining children in care and exercising control through an insistence on long-term fostering does not enable families to cope better with difficulties or ensure the permanency and successful outcome of placements. There is simply no evidence that this is so, and social workers must be honest enough to recognise their own anxieties in determining why they sometimes resist handing over responsibility and control to new parents. Our central concern must be to safeguard the welfare of children. In order to do this, we must pay attention to what children tell us, in all kinds of ways, about their hopes, fears, wishes and feelings. Decision-making is a risky business. Social workers do not have absolute knowledge. However, we should have well-developed skills of observation, communication, analysis, and an ability to assess likely outcomes in terms of present knowledge and information about particular cases. It is unrealistic to avoid making decisions about adoption because we cannot *guarantee* success, provided that appropriate use is made of available knowledge and skills.

Agency procedure: the adoption panel

I have not spent much time discussing procedures or statutory requirements with regard to family placement, because the former will be influenced by the particular structure and policies of individual agencies and the latter are clearly spelled out elsewhere. However, every local authority or voluntary society which places children in accordance with the Adoption Agencies Regulations must have an Adoption Panel. In practice such Panels have commonly been used to consider matters relating to permanent family placement, including adoption and fostering. Membership is usually drawn from different professional and management groups with medical and legal specialists in attendance. It is likely that the new Regulations, which are expected shortly, will specify the composition of Panels in more detail. In the context of our present discussion, I am concerned about the way in which Panels have been used as part of agency procedure, and the impact of this on successful family placement. Great emphasis has always been placed on individual work with applicants who wish to foster or adopt and presentation of their applications to an agency's Panel. My own research indicated that intensive work with applicants was geared to the Panel's eventual decision, that following this there was little contact with prospective adoptive or foster parents prior to place-ment, and that such approval implicitly denoted an expectation of good parenting. I have already drawn the reader's attention to the problematic nature of deciding whether, in the absence of any particular link with a child, applicants have the necessary qualities or characteristics to ensure their ability as foster parents or adopters. Additionally, knowing that acceptance or rejection depends on a social worker's assessment and a Panel's decision inevitably brings into play all those difficulties associated with a selection model, presentation of self for 'approval', and impression management.

A report published by the Department of Health and Social Security (1979) points to a lack of understanding about the present *statutory* duties of an Adoption Panel. The report was written prior to certain amendments to the Regulations when Panels were termed 'case committees'. It states that

> it is not certain whether the functions of the case committee are always fully understood. Its statutory duty is to decide that a particular home is suitable for a specific child. It may in addition consider the availability of children for adoption as well as the suitability of adopters in general and other matters relating to adoptions. This confusion is probably not confined to the par-ticipating agencies and it therefore needs consideration.

(DHSS, 1979, p. 16)

Singleton (1979) makes the same point when discussing the possibil-ity of appeals against a Panel's decision.

At the moment there is no statutory requirement for a Panel to approve applications from prospective adopters and foster parents. My research clearly showed that the use of the Panel for this purpose was detrimental to co-operation, openness of communication, and the development of trust between applicants and social workers. It may also introduce an artificial barrier into the adoption and fostering process which is likely to inhibit continued learning and suggests, mistakenly, that most of the vital work has been accomplished prior to approval. Increasing efforts to place older and handicapped children with adoptive families have not only raised questions about the use of social work resources and the timing of intensive work with appli-cants, but have also led some practitioners to examine the validity of assessment, preparation, and approval, *in isolation from the needs and characteristics of a particular child*.

Phyllida Sawbridge comments in the first annual report of 'Parents for Children' that part of the preparation and decision making as to whether people can take on the adoptive role seems to us of necessity related to a particular child. The children's needs are so varied that we do not see how we could approve people in the abstract as potential parents – it makes much more sense to approve the placement of one particular child with one particular family and this is what we ask our committee to do.

('Parents for Children', 1976–7, p. 5)

Sawbridge suggests that this approach has led to children being placed with applicants who would normally be considered 'unsuitable' by other agencies working within more conventional procedural limits. She acknowledges that sometimes social workers and applicants may disagree about whether the latter can cope with the challenges of parenting a particular child and that self-selection cannot always be a determining factor. Working in this way was, and I am sure still is, viewed by many agencies as unconventional and probably unacceptable. This is conceded by Sawbridge and she appreciates that 'this approach may shock some people. Many social workers would not dream of discussing a child with people who have not been formally approved' (Sawbridge, 1978, p. 13).

The results of my own research and the views of some practitioners from specialist home-finding agencies suggest that an emphasis on the Adoption Panel's role in accepting or rejecting applications, without reference to linking, has clear disadvantages. There may be some cases where applicants do not voluntarily withdraw or appropriately self-select but where they do not appear to have the necessary tolerance, flexibility, commitment, and most importantly, willingness to learn and work with an agency, for the placement of a child with special needs. Individual social workers have recourse to their senior consultative staff and team members in deciding whether prospective adopters or foster parents should be asked to withdraw an application. Any worries may be discussed with the Panel at an early stage, or if applicants think that an agency has misjudged them, there is no reason why the Panel cannot consider the case and question a social worker's decision.

At the time of writing, it is not possible to state how the matter of 'approval' will be dealt with in the revised version of the Adoption Agencies Regulations. In any event, we must try to achieve the kind of procedure, including the use of an Adoption (and Fostering) Panel, which takes into account the detrimental aspects of assessment and selection, and facilitates a preparation model of working with an emphasis on learning, linking families and children and post-placement support.

Conclusion

The reader may have noted an absence of remarks concerning what agencies and social workers should do about applications to foster or adopt which are rejected. They may, however, appreciate by now that I would question the apparently straightforward relationship between assessment, selection, acceptance or rejection of applications, and the model of working on which this is based. Given that many agencies still take what Sawbridge would call a 'conventional' approach to approving applications and that we may, hopefully infrequently, wish to encourage applicants to withdraw, I recognise that it would be unrealistic to ignore or deny the significance of this subject. The nine adoption agencies participating in my research did not consider it their responsibility to provide explanations to applicants in cases of rejection, and I suspect that this policy is widespread. Reasons given for holding this position were that first, since much information on which decisions are based is confidential, this could not be passed on by way of explanation. Secondly, where couples are considered unsuitable for social, psychological, or emotional reasons, they might be unable to comprehend the nature of professional judgements, or if they did understand these, they might be emotionally damaged by such revelations.

Some writers have recognised that an agency's unwillingness to explain a social worker's or Panel's decision may engender feelings of self-doubt, lack of confidence, mutual blame as family members try to sort out who said the wrong thing or gave a poor impression. Or if applicants respond to rejection by feeling angry and resentful, they may continue to contact other agencies in the hope of finally achieving approval. Waters does not accept that the confidentiality of medical information necessarily prohibits explanations in the event of rejection. He suggests that the applicants' general practitioner 'may be willing to discuss with the agency's medical adviser the best way to tell the prospective adopters that they have not been accepted, so that adequate explanation can be given rather than leaving untold doubts in their minds' (Waters, 1977, p. 161). Rowe is very clear about the position if applications are rejected on what are assessed to be social or emotional grounds. She suggests that social workers must help applicants to understand why adoption is inadvisable for them and goes on to assert that, explanations must be based on what the applicants themselves tell us, not on our own intuition or on interpretations of their underlying attitudes . . . We do not have the right to risk upsetting a marriage, to breakdown people's defences and make them more unhappy. But people usually feel better if they have a chance to defend their position and also to gain a better understanding of themselves.   (Rowe, 1966, p. 191)

We might have expected Jane Rowe to hold such an enlightened view in 1966, but this is unfortunately not the case for many agencies and social workers operating in the field today.

The knowledge that their applications would be considered by a, then, case committee, that there existed a possibility of being rejected, and that in this event no explanation could be expected, held considerable significance for the prospective adopters in my research population and influenced the way in which they approached contact with social workers. They commented, 'You are entitled to know. You try to be helpful and informative to them and they should be the same back to you', and 'I would be very upset – after all the vetting and assessing they do on you, the least they could do is explain why they have turned you down – surely they owe you that much.' There were many more remarks in the same vein and there is no reason to suppose that my respondents comprised an atypical group. This serves to bring us back to the importance of trust and honesty throughout social workers' contact with prospective adopters and foster parents. In effect it makes the job harder because we must be able and willing to explain decisions without recourse to élite professional judgements and interpretations, or feelings and intuition, which applicants' are supposed not to comprehend. We must apply analysis to our own thoughts and decisions as well as to external problems. If social workers fail to take this approach, their help may be viewed as unacceptable and their facilitating, educative, and supportive role will be lost to children and new families.

7
Conclusion: Getting It All Together

To be sure, an ordinary passer-by would think that my rose looked just like you – the rose that belongs to me. But in herself alone she is more important than all the hundreds of you other roses: because it is she that I have watered; because it is she that I have put under the glass globe; because it is she that I have sheltered behind the screen; because it is for her that I have killed the caterpillars; because it is she that I have listened to, when she grumbled, or boasted, or even sometimes when she said nothing. Because she is *my* rose.

Antoine de Saint-Exupery, *The Little Prince*

Introduction

It is not the purpose of this chapter to summarise previous discussions or information and it must be accepted that any single attempt to contribute to knowledge and understanding cannot attend to all the questions, or indeed provide all the answers, which the hopeful reader might expect. Writing in 1964, Krugman noted that,

> in fact, the field of adoption seems now to be so characterised by outspokenness, rapid growth and change that new programmes are in existence before old ones have been evaluated; or that while we are engrossed in the struggle to achieve change it has occurred almost without our awareness . . . we can anticipate that diversity of opinion, variation in theoretical approaches and action programmes, and a high level of community interest will continue to characterise this field.
> (Krugman, 1964, p. 268)

Krugman's remarks are as pertinent now as they were in 1964. Although this book may be viewed as a contribution to what will surely be a continuing debate, it is not intended to provide easy or comfortable 'take it or leave it' options. I have argued the case for adoption and attempted to consider the practice implications of working with children and families towards this end. If the reader holds a contrary view, then I hope that the contents of this book will facilitate an informed and constructive level of criticism and dialogue.

Permanency and adoption

In Chapter 1 I referred to the current debate between those who favour adoption as a way of ensuring security for children who cannot return home, and those who criticise this approach on a number of grounds. The critics' opposition largely rests on three major areas of disagreement. First, deriving from an ideological position, they argue that the class and value bias of those who formulate and implement the law effectively discriminates against parents whose children come into care and who are likely to be relatively powerless in terms of knowledge and social and economic resources. Schorr (1978), for example, has described adoption as 'a system for distributing children from the poor to the middle class', and Holman (1976 and 1980) accused the 1975 Children Act of concentrating 'exclusively on facilitating the remoal of children from their families and on reducing the rights of the natural parents'. Poor parenting is thus largely viewed as a result of social deprivation and its associated pressures on families. Secondly, and related to the above position, the critics argue in terms of policy and professional practice that insufficient attention has been given to the prevention of family breakdown and admission to care and that social workers too frequently fail to consider parents' wishes, to involve them in decision-making, and to recognise their rights. Thirdly, it is suggested that the cessation of parental contact and lack of biological continuity inherent in adoption is likely to be detrimental to the social and emotional development of adopted children.

Many of those who favour planning for permanence are sympathetic to the arguments of their critics. They have asserted loudly and clearly that such planning must proceed from the basis of substantial improvements in preventive and rehabilitative services at resource, policy and practice levels. Neither would they condone social work intervention in family life which neglects the needs and rights of parents and their children or dismisses continuing contact between them where the former continue to function as 'psychological parents'. It is further accepted and amply demonstrated that a proportion of admissions to care are associated with social and economic disadvantage. However, it must be said that, first, whatever our ideological inclinations, we are required to make decisions about children within the present legal, economic and social structure. Secondly, biological relatedness does not guarantee mutually rewarding parent–child relationships. To hold the view that social and economic disadvantage is the root cause of disharmony and breakdown in family relationships belies the complexity of this area and does little service to parents who are unwilling or unable to develop parenting skills or to their children who are subject to distorted, destructive, or inconsistent interaction with their parents. Thirdly, the supposed dangers of substituting legal and social ties for biological continuity do not appear to be invariably consequent upon adoption. Fourthly, we should remember that no one has inalienable rights without regard for the rights of others and reference to socially prescribed and legally protected expectations of behaviour. Parental rights are no different and are not called into question unless they can be demonstrated to threaten, in this context, the individual rights of children. Attempting to balance the rights of parents and their children is not *in itself* reprehensible, neither does it contravene the commonly accepted principles which inform justice in this society. Criticism of the 1975 Children Act may assume validity if parents are prevented from exercising their rights because they are disadvantaged by structural inequalities in our society or by a professional abuse of power.

It is now accepted that social workers have a responsibility to look beyond the problems of individual clients and to exert pressure collectively for social change. This point is not at issue. This book, however, is written for social workers who must make decisions now and who must do so within the framework of competing ideological arguments, political and economic constraints, limited knowledge and legally circumscribed choices. I have to conclude on balance that adoption must reasonably be viewed as an important alternative for children who cannot grow up with their biological parents.

Foster and adoptive parents: clients or . . . ?

I hesitate to comment on this question because the language which must be used implies so many value judgements, and begs so many questions, about the social status and rights of those whom we call clients. However, I cannot avoid reaching some conclusions about this matter. A client is someone who requests or needs a service. Those who express an interest in becoming foster or adoptive parents have the peculiarly dual nature of initially requesting, but later providing, a specific kind of service. Much of this book has been concerned to spell out the service which social workers should provide to prospective foster and adoptive parents, and the nature of the relationship which should inform this undertaking. I have emphasised the importance of continuing social work help after children are placed with new families, and where appropriate, following adoption.

When some social workers refer to the client status of foster and adoptive parents they unfortunately assume that the latter have problems which must be investigated, and define ensuing relationships on the basis of professional distance and unequal control over information and decision-making. It should be recognised that this approach has been questioned in relation to *any* clients with whom social workers are in contact. Attempting to understand a client's perception of his world, sharing information, open-communication, working to agreed contracts, and consulting over important decisions, have all been given explicit attention. Social workers should not see their role in terms of doing things *to* clients, but in relation to working *with* clients towards agreed goals. Clearly this is not always possible and, as we know, parents may not always concur with plans for their children's future or be able to argue their case effectively. However, this demonstrates rather than undermines the importance of the propositions outlined above.

My own views about foster and adoptive parents as 'clients' should be clear. Yes, they are clients in the sense that they require a service which will prepare them to carry out specific tasks and will support them while they are doing so. However, this does not imply that foster and adoptive parents should, at any stage, be deprived of access to information and real involvement in decision-making. As I have noted, there are many critics of the 'professional mystique' who reasonably argue that these principles should provide the framework for *all* social worker–client interaction, no matter what the particular circumstances.

My approach is summed up by Phyllida Sawbridge in her introduction to 'Opening New Doors', a booklet based on talks by Kay Donley of Spaulding for Children. She says that Donley

is challenging us to come out from behind our desks, where we sit hemmed in by narrow concepts of what constitutes professional practice, and to start really working *with* children and *with* adoptive parents. What applicants need and want is preparation and help in the task which they are offering to take on: vetting (an English word quite new to Mrs Donley and one with which she never quite came to terms), is a judgemental process based on the obviously unfounded belief that a social worker can really get to know a couple in three or four interviews and can make a realistic prediction about their ability to parent an unknown child. Mrs Donley asks us to drop such unrealistic notions, and to start from the quite different angle of assuming that most people are capable of deciding for themselves whether or not they can take on a given task, provided (and this is the key) they are fully informed as to what may be involved and are offered adequate support in doing it.

(Donley, 1975, p. 8)

The nature of adoption

I hope the reader is still with me since our understanding of the nature of adoption is essential to making decisions about children, working with prospective adoptive parents, and the social and legal context in which these activities take place. The differences between biological and adoptive parenthood, and the difficulties for the latter and their adopted children which these are presumed to entail, have already been mentioned. As we know Kirk (1964) has contributed to this discussion by elucidating two coping mechanisms for adoptive parents: 'rejection of difference' or 'acknowledgement of difference'. The latter involves continued and explicit reminders that children have joined their new families through adoption. There are two major factors which must be considered here; the first concerns the social arrangement of adoption, and the second relates to how this may be handled in order to enhance the probability of successful outcome.

First, then, how may we assess the significance of the social, rather than biological, basis of adoptive relationships? Much of the apparent confusion about this matter (including that of David Kirk) relates to a failure to distinguish between the biological fact of reproduction and the social activity of parenting. I have argued elsewhere (1980), and with reference to the research and analysis of Busfield and Paddon (1977), that human reproduction must be considered in relation to social action; the *desire* for parenthood is socially as well as biologically grounded. Men and women, as intentional and social beings, engage in action which has meaning for them, rather than simply behaving in a biologically determined way which is largely independent of social mediation. An approach to understanding parenthood and parenting which emphasises social action and meaning, clearly distinguishes between biological reproduction and the meaning of parenthood and activity of parenting. Furthermore, the core process of social interaction between parents and their children may be described analytically in terms of the 'social construction of reality'.

Adoptive parents and children are brought together in a taken-for-granted world with a common stock of knowledge and institutionalised roles defining the rights and obligations of parenthood and the expectations which parents and children share about family life. Although such knowledge exists it does not prescribe, in detail, how parents and children should feel or behave towards each other. It is through a continuing process of social exchange, interpretation, common experience, and mutual understanding, that parents and children construct their own version of reality and continually confirm this through day-to-day conversations and activities. This reality is not pre-given. Because it is socially constructed, it is emergent and open to modification, although it develops within the framework of an already available stock of knowledge and social structure. As this constructed reality is continually confirmed and reinforced through conversation with significant others, it is likely to become more stable because forms of interaction become habitualised and knowledge becomes shared and taken for granted. In their analysis of marriage Berger and Kellner describe the process thus; 'reconstructed present and reinterpreted past are perceived as a continuum, extended forwards into a commonly projected future' (Berger and Kellner, 1970, p. 63). For children who are adopted as babies, the social construction of reality will depend on interaction, with their adoptive parents as significant others. Where older children are joining new families the construction of a shared reality will be more problematic, since the former will arrive with their own experiences and expectations deriving from previous relationships, different significant others, and habitualised forms of interaction. Failure to construct an area of shared reality reflects the possible dissatisfaction of adoptive parents and difficulties in the social and emotional adjustment of adopted children.

The above discussion brings us to the conclusion that the *essential* difference between biological and adoptive parenthood lies with the matter of reproduction; not with the desire to be parents or the activity of parenting which are grounded in social action. Kadushin illustrates this point when he says, on the basis of his research, that

parenthood is a *social role* demanding of the parent a complex series of repetitive behaviours . . . The non-adoptive parent caring for his child and the adoptive parent caring for his child are functionally engaged in the same sort of behaviours, are encountering the same problems, reacting in the same ways, and are, for the most part, indistinguishable from each other. Hence there is no difference perceived.   (Kadushin, 1970a, p. 13)

The reader may be beginning to suspect that I would espouse the validity of 'rejection of difference' and therefore encourage adoptive parents to deny the reality of their peculiar status. I must say quite clearly that this is *not* the case. However, what I have tried to do is to clarify the essential nature of this difference, given the vital place which it has occupied in discussions about adoption. My position is that a rejection of difference, as this pertains to the social aspects of parenthood and parenting, is quite consistent with recognising the reality of a child and family's adoptive status. This is based on the empirical observation that the genesis of adoptive families is different from that of others, but that the meaning of parenthood and family relationships is not. As Kadushin again observes,

the crucial distinguishing factor with regard to the assumption of the role of parents is in the past. Only a limited, albeit significant, sector of life has been involved and it involves a non-recurrent act . . . The sense of parenthood has been developed and reinforced by habituation and close association between parents and children. *The fact of adoption is not denied, it merely loses its significance.*

(Kadushin, 1970b, p. 13, my emphasis)

This brings us to the second part of the question, relating to adoption outcome. Kirk (1964) argues that 'acknowledgement of difference' is vital to successful adoption arrangements and that prospective adopters must be prepared to cope with the dilemmas of their essentially peculiar role. I would suggest that continued reminders of a child's adoptive status are not conducive to successful outcome and that Kirk's approach is in danger of undermining adopters' perceptions of themselves as 'real' parents and the validity of adoptive relationships. There is some evidence to support this argument. First, Witmer (1963) comments that respondents' denial of any problems, particularly arising from the adoption of their children, was *not* associated with relatively poor adoption outcome. Jaffee and Fanshel (1970) remark that the majority of their respondents denied having any difficulties which were connected with the nature of adoptive relationships. Secondly, the views of adoptive parents referred to by Jaffee and Fanshel were largely confirmed when the authors interviewed a sample of the formers' adopted children, who were aged between twenty-one and thirty at the time of this study (see Jaffee, 1974). From his follow-up research of older children who were placed for adoption, Kadushin (1970a) found that where adoptive parents were self-conscious about their status and ambivalent about accepting adopted children as full members of their families, this was related to poorer outcome. Thirdly, several researchers have noted that when and how children are told about adoption seems to be less important for outcome than the quality of family relationships and communication which provide the context of such a disclosure.

Fourthly, it has been confirmed several times over that adoptees' satisfaction with family and parental relationships depends on their perception that they were accepted and reared as if they had been born into their adoptive families. McWhinnie (1967) notes that the adoptees in her study wanted to be told of their status but did *not* want frequent discussion of it at home or outside the family and that 'they wanted to feel that their position in their adoptive family was exactly that of a biological son or daughter'. More recently Raynor (1980) comments about her sample of adult adoptees that 'when they felt they had been treated as though they had been born into the family four in five were well adjusted'. Triseliotis comments that adoptees in his study who were dissatisfied with their experience and attempting to locate their biological parents, were those who said that they had 'felt unloved or distant from their parents and who did not feel they belonged' (Triseliotis, 1973, p. 62).

Despite publicity preceding the implementation of Section 26 of the Children Act (access to birth records) and the expected demand for counselling, it would appear that only a small minority of adoptees have acted upon their new legal rights. Leeding (1980) collected information about adoptees making inquiries to several local authorities and Day (1980) reported on the first 500 counselling interviews conducted at the General Register Office. Day notes that the proportion of adopted adults affected by the legislation, who requested counselling as a preliminary to obtaining their original birth certificates, was far less than expected and between 1 per cent and 2 per cent only. There was some evidence that adoptees who had been unhappy in their adoptive families were more likely to be intent on tracing their biological parents, a point which was also made by Triseliotis. However, both Leeding and Day comment that the vast majority of adoptees seemed to be mature and well adjusted and that they showed considerable loyalty to their adoptive parents.

Adoptees seeking access to their birth records wanted to complete the picture of their biological parents and to fill in the gap between conception and joining their adoptive families. For the purposes of our analysis we may conclude that provided relationships are good, adoptees will come to view their adoptive parents as the significant people in their lives and as their 'real' parents, just as they wish to feel as though they had been born into their adoptive families.

Fifthly, Triscliotis (1983) reports on follow-up research which contrasts particular areas of outcome for people who grew up adopted and those who grew up in long-term foster homes. At the time of his study, the forty-four adoptees were largely in their mid-twenties and the forty former foster children were in their early twenties. He concludes,

> compared to those who grew up in long-term fostering, adoptees in general appeared more confident and secure with fewer doubts about themselves and their capacity to cope with life. With very few exceptions, the adoptees' identification with their adoptive families was complete with none of the ambiguities found in the fostering situation. Whilst adoptees had no doubts about belonging to their adoptive families and the family belonging to them, many of those fostered were aware that their legal position was unclear and that their lives could have been disturbed at any stage during the placement.   (Triseliotis, 1983, p. 30)

It would seem from these observations that successful adoption outcome is related to a sense of security and belonging in family relationships, and the ability of adopters to talk about background and biological parents without allowing this to interfere with a child's perception that he is accepted and loved *as if* he had been born into his adoptive family. Helping children grow up into competent adults also presupposes an element of discipline and control. On this topic Raynor asserts that

> during the course of the study it became increasingly clear to the interviewers that parents who had little feeling of entitlement to their child – for whatever reason – were often incapable of disciplining him. Such people felt they had little right to the child, that in spite of the legal ties that bound them to him there were stronger ties which still bound him to his birth mother, and if they overstepped by denying him anything he wanted or by disciplining him in other ways he might withdraw his love for them and seek his

other mother. This fear seemed to be far more prevalent than adoption workers realise and its consequences could be disastrous.

(Raynor, 1980, p. 109)

Similar comments have also been made by other researchers.

In essence, those factors which would appear to be important for successful adoption outcome, depend on the ability of adoptive parents to feel secure about the validity of their parenting role and to perceive themselves as a child's 'real' parents. The view that a self-conscious awareness of 'difference' may exacerbate difficulties in the adoptive relationship has been supported by Rothenberg *et al.* (1971) and by Rowe (1971).

Social work in adoption must therefore be based on the acceptance of two essential propositions. First, social work intervention must focus on helping prospective adopters to decide whether they are able and willing to cope with the additional tasks imposed by adoptive parenthood, must prepare them to deal appropriately with these tasks, and must support them while they are building their new families. Particular information, preparation and the time scale involved in providing support, will depend on the kinds of children who are being placed for adoption. Secondly, the recognition that adoption involves additional parental tasks must *not* be confused with the message that adoptive parenthood is less valid or less 'real' then biological parenthood, or that it is *inherently* problematic simply because it is based on a socially contrived arrangement. If social workers are ambivalent about either of these two propositions, they are unlikely to work in such a way as to facilitate successful adoption outcome or to enable adopters to develop sufficient security in their role as parents to handle the reality and associated tasks of adoptive parenthood.

Concluding remarks

From a child's point of view the advantages of adoption lie in safeguarding the security and continuity of relationships with psychological parents. Adoption also bestows social and legal recognition of parenthood. If adoptive parents are prepared for their role in the way which I have suggested, they should feel able to perceive themselves as a child's 'real' parents, and in relation to this, to feel sufficiently confident and secure to talk about biological parents, a child's background, and circumstances leading to an adoption placement. Adoption does not deny the importance of biological parents and significant others, but should provide the security for children and their adoptive parents to accept, understand and refer to past events and experiences.

Given this approach, there is no insurmountable reason why the idea of 'open adoption' should not be further explored in this country. Baran *et al*. (1976) has discussed the benefits of open adoption where the security of adoptive relationships is able to accommodate continuing links and contact with significant people from the child's past and biological family. In other situations where open adoption is culturally supported, for example in Hawaii, the Cook Islands, and among the Eskimos of North Alaska, it would seem that the adopter's parental role is acknowledged and safeguarded and there does not appear to be any confusion about the rights, obligations, and duties of adoptive and biological parents. Neither is there any evidence of insecurity on the part of adoptive parents and their children. However, the significance of adoption remains important and any contact between children and significant others outside the adoptive family would, in the context of this discussion, be evaluated in relation to the kinds of factors already mentioned in previous chapters.

Any discussion about adoption must take into account the legal, ideological, and social nature of this arrangement. Social work practice must refer to personal values, cultural norms, the legal framework in which decisions are made, knowledge derived from empirical data and its interpretation, and day-to-day interaction with clients. I hope that this book will help to sharpen the edges of debate and clarify social workers' understanding of how and why they make particular decisions, choose specific methods of intervention, and develop appropriate skills.

A Guide to Further Reading

Chapter 1   Adoption in context and social work intervention

Short historical accounts of the development of adoption practice and legislation may be found in Benet (1976), Tizard (1977), Triseliotis (1970). Two publications from British Agencies For Adoption and Fostering, *Fostering in the 70s and Beyond* (1977) and *Adoption in the 70s* (1976), provide an excellent overview of changes in policy and practice, and relevant research. The former pamphlet is in the process of being updated. Although not the focus of this book, the plight of childless couples seeking to adopt babies has been given considerable attention. Readers interested in this topic may find the following literature helpful: Eck Menning (1977), Humphrey (1969), Houghton and Houghton (1977), Renne, (1977). An extensive guide to development of specialist fostering and adoption resources is provided by Cooper (1978), Shaw and Hipgrave (1982) and Triseliotis (1980). If readers have an interest in child care, adoption legislation and its implications, I would recommend Rawstron (1980), Freeman (1981), an excellent paper by White (1980), a further paper by White (1982) on wardship proceedings, and Holden (1982). The 'Legal Notes' published regularly in *Adoption and Fostering* are a constant source of information and new understanding. My references to child care programmes in the USA have been highly summarised and for further details I would suggest recourse to Adcock (1980b) and Prosser (1978). A full account of the Lothian approach is provided by McKay (1980). For a full discussion of the pros and cons of independently arranged adoptions it would be worthwhile to have a look at the Hurst Report (Home Office, 1954), the Houghton Report (Scottish Home Dept., 1972), Triseliotis (1970), and Witmer *et al.*'s (1963) research on independent adoptions in the United States. If readers are interested in David Kirk's analysis, further research and discussion of his approach may be found in Toussieng (1971), and Sensel and Yeakel (1970). The problems of selecting adopters within the broad range of 'normal' functioning has been explored by Fanshel (1962 and 1972). Where there are few guidelines for the selection of prospective adopters and foster parents it has been demonstrated that social workers do make different decisions and use personal values and 'rule of thumb' methods as a basis for choice; see Brieland (1959), Brown and Brieland (1975), Bradley (1966), Soothill and Derbyshire (1981), and Soothill (1982). Some attention has been given to how the recipients of social work help perceive their interaction with social workers and the usefulness of their advice and assistance; Mayer and

Timms (1970) is of course the classic study on this topic, followed by Timms (1973), and latterly Page and Clark's (1977) and Kahan's (1979) edition of youngsters' comments about being in care. Cook (1982) makes out a convincing case that social workers should listen more carefully to clients' assessments of their own needs.

Chapter 2   Is blood thicker than water?

The text of Chapter 2 only includes reference to major follow-up studies and the reader may wish to consult further literature. For a follow-up study of illegitimate children, born and subsequently adopted in Germany, and aged twenty-five to thirty years old at the time of the last assessment, see Zur Nieden (1951). The often quoted research of Skodak and Skeels (1949) concentrates on the intellectual development of adopted children as compared to the IQ of their biological parents. Fisch *et al.* (1970) compared the progress of ninety-four children adopted by non-relatives with that of fifty children who remained with their biological mothers and were later jointly adopted by their mothers and stepfathers. Several studies have attempted to assess the occurrence, degree and type of psychopathology in adoptees and have related these findings to the existence of similar psychopathology in biological and/or adoptive parents, in an effort to disentangle the influence of hereditary and environmental factors; see Cunningham *et al.* (1975), Cadoret *et al.* (1975), Cadoret *et al.* (1976), Braftos *et al.* (1968), Goodwin *et al.* (July 1977) and (September 1977), Morrison and Stewart (1973), Rosenthal *et al.* (1975). Readers may like to have a look at Tizard's (1977) research which created quite a stir when it was published. She compared the development of a group of adopted children with that of illegitimate children living with their biological mothers, both groups of children having previously spent a period in residental care. For a fuller account of Gill and Jackson's research on transracial adoption, readers are referred to their recently published book (1983). The practice of transracial adoption in the United States and follow-up research data is discussed by Simon and Altstein (1977) and (1981). See also Harvey (1982) for information about transracial adoption in Australia. Although not strictly the subject of this book, Triseliotis' (1978) follow-up study of children who spent between seven and fifteen years each in a single foster home makes interesting reading.

For a review of the methodology and findings of research concerned with the differences between infertile and fertile couples, readers should have a look at Seward *et al.* (1965), Mai *et al.* (1972a), Karahasanoglu *et al.* (1972). Folklore about the relationship between adoption and subsequent conception is so widely expressed that readers might like to explore this further. Reference should be made to Weinstein (1962), Rock *et al.* (1965), Weir and Weir (1966), Arronet *et al.* (1974), Smith (1980). Sorosky *et al.* (1975) provide a detailed review of the literature about identity problems in adoptees and the psycho-analytic approach reflected in family romance themes, the Oedipal crisis, and biological discontinuity. The debate about transracial adoption and loss of racial identity has been going on in the United States for sometime and is well documented by Simon and Altstein (1977). The Steering Group of the *Soul Kids Campaign* (1977) reports on one of the first concerted attempts in Britain to find racially matched families for children needing family placement.

Chapter 3   Making plans and choosing resources

For a practice oriented and summarised guide to decision-making in adoption with helpful diagrams, flow charts, work sheets, and so on, see Mackay (1982). BASW (1977) has, of course, produced a document which attempts to define the rights of children. There is an enormous amount of literature on child development, but for manageable reading I would suggest Clarke and Clarke (1976), Pilling and Kellmer-Pringle (1978), and Fahlberg (1982). Classic studies which document foster parents' perceptions of their role are those by Adamson (1973) and George (1970). Further light is thrown upon this matter by Trasler (1960) and Shaw *et al.* (1975). Parker (1980) and his colleagues on the working party provide a very balanced discussion of issues related to planning for children in care. Timms and Timms (1977) make some incisive and probably unpopular comments about how social workers make decisions and their tendency to transform matters of cognition into matters of feeling.

Chapter 4   Parents and children

Working with biological parents is given attention by Tod (1971), the Advisory Council on Child Care (1970), the Working Party on Fostering Practice (1976), and Simms and Smith (1982). For helpful and practice-oriented discussions of working with children, readers should refer to appropriate chapters in Unger *et al.* (1977), Jewett (1978), and Fitzgerald *et al.* (1982). Ryan and Walker (1983) have produced an excellent and highly readable guide to working with children with an emphasis on practice. In this context it is worth referring to Mann (1977), Curtis' (1982) discussion of communication through play, and Jefferies and Gillespie's (1981) article on art therapy.

Chapter 5   Working with family resources

Donley (1975) provides a lively and manageable account of 'Spaulding for Children's' approach to recruiting and working with prospective adopters. The literature on group work with applicants is now becoming extensive. I would suggest some easily digestible articles for readers who are interested in this topic; see for practice in the United States, Wiehe (1972), Anderson and Kaufman (1973), Goodridge (1975), and in Britain, Reid (1973), Bayley

(1975), Horne (1981), and Short and Gray (1982). There is a useful section on this subject in Kerrane *et al.*'s (1980) account of work in the Barnardo's New Families Project. Many enlightening articles on working with prospective foster and adoptive families will be found in *Adoption and Fostering*, the quarterly journal of British Agencies for Adoption and Fostering. A must for prospective adopters of older children is Jewett's (no date) pamphlet, 'For Ever and Ever' which is compiled from material written by adoptive parents. For a summary of recent research and approaches to the recruitment and training of foster parents, see National Children's Bureau (1983). Heim (1982) considers adoption from the perspective of an adoptive parent. Disruption of placements is considered by Fitzgerald (1983).

Chapter 6   Getting families and children together

For some indication of research on similarities between adoptees and their adoptive parents see Fisch *et al.* (1970), Garn *et al.* (1976), and Grotevant *et al.* (1977). Finding racially matched families for children is discussed by Fitzgerald and James (1981), Schroeder and Lightfoot (1983). There are also some useful articles on this subject in Churchill *et al.* (1979). Post-adoption work is considered by Erikson (1961), and Picton and Seager (1977). Fahlberg (1981) has written a useful account of how to help children when they must move.

Chapter 7   Conclusion: Getting it all together

The whole question of natural rights, society, and personal freedom is extremely complicated and relates to the discussion of legal and social philosophers. This book is clearly not the place to look at this topic in any detail but some useful introductory material may be found in d'Entreves (1951), Hart (1967), Berlin (1967), and Locke (1959). Readers who are interested in exploring the significance of meaning and the social construction of reality should start off with Berger (1963), Berger and Luckmann (1966), Berger and Kellner (1970), Natanson (1970), and Busfield and Paddon (1977). There is some informative discussion about open adoption in Benet (1976), Ringwood (1976) and Ferguson (1981).

Bibliography

Adamson, G. (1973) *The Caretakers*, London, Bookstall Publications.

Adcock, M. (1980a) 'The Right to Permanent Placement', *Adoption and Fostering*, 99, pp. 21–4.

Adcock, M. (1980b) 'Social Work Dilemmas', in Adcock *et al.* (eds), *Terminating Parental Contact*, London, BAAF, pp. 14–24.

Adcock, M. (1981) 'The Right of a Child to a Permanent Placement', *Rights of Children*, London, BAAF, pp. 19–29.

Adrian, R. J. *et al.* (1966) 'Linear Discriminant Function Classification of Accepted and Rejected Adoptive Parents', *Journal of Clinical Psychology*, vol. 27, no. 2, pp. 251–4.

Advisory Council on Child Care (1970) *A Guide to Adoption Practice*, London, HMSO.

Anderson, H. W. and Kaufman, S. J. (1973) 'The Group Method in Adoption of Children with Special Needs', *Child Welfare*, vol. 52, no. 1, pp. 45–51.

Andrews, R. G. (1963) 'Casework Methodology with Adoptive Applicant Couples', *Child Welfare*, vol. 42, no. 10, pp. 488–92.

Andrews, R. G. (1970) 'Adoption and the Resolution of Infertility', *Fertility and Sterility*, vol. 21, no. 1, pp. 73–6.

Arronet, G. H. *et al.* (1974) 'The Influence of Adoption on Subsequent Pregnancy in Infertile Marriage', *International Journal of Infertility*, 19, pp. 159–62.

Association of Directors of Social Services (1976) *Implementation Notes: Children Act 1975* ADSS.

Baran, A. *et al.* (1976) 'Open Adoption', *Social Work*, vol. 21, pp. 97–100.

Bass, C. (1975) 'Matchmaker-Matchmaker: Older Child Adoption Failures', *Child Welfare*, vol. LIV, no. 7, pp. 505–12.

Bayley, N. (1975) 'Homefinding for older Children and the Use of Groups', *Child Adoption*, 81, pp. 25–8.

Benet, M. K. (1976) *The Character of Adoption*, London, Jonathan Cape.

Berger, P. L. (1963) *Invitation to Sociology*, London, Penguin.

Berger, P. L. and Kellner, A. (1970) 'Marriage and the Construction of Reality', in Dreitzel, H. P. (ed.) *Recent Sociology: No. 2*, London, Collier-Macmillan.

Berger, P. L. and Luckmann, T. (1966) *The Social Construction of Reality*, London, Penguin.

Berlin, I. (1967) 'Two Concepts of Liberty', in Quinton, A. (ed.), *Political Philosophy*, Oxford, Oxford University Press, pp. 141–53.

Bohman, M. (1970) *Adopted Children and their Families*, Stockholm, Proprius.

Borgatta, E. F. and Fanshel, D. (1965) *Behaviour Characteristics of Children known to Psychiatric Outpatients Clinics*, New York, CWLA.

Bowerbank, M. W. (1970) 'The Case Committee – What is its Future?', *Child Adoption*, no. 59, pp. 35–8.

Braden, J. A. (1970) 'Adoption in a Changing World', *Social Casework*, vol. 50, no. 8, pp. 486–90.

Bradley, T. (1966) *An Exploration of Caseworkers' Perceptions of Adoption Applicants*, New York, Child Welfare League of America.

Braftos, O. *et al.* (1968) 'Mental Illness and Crime in Adopted Children and Adoptive Parents', *Acta Psychiatrica Scand Danem*, 44, 4, pp. 376–84.

Brenner, R. F. (1951) *A Follow-Up Study of Adoptive Families*, New York, Child Adoption Research Committee Inc.

Brieland, D. (1959) *The Selection of Adoptive Parents at Intake*, New York, Child Welfare League of America.

British Association of Social Workers (1977) 'Children in Care: A BASW Charter of Rights', *Social Work Today*, 8, 25 pp. 7–9.

Brown, E. G. and Brieland, D. (1975) 'Adoptive Screening', *Social Work*, vol. 20, pp. 291–5.

Busfield, J. and Paddon, M. (1977) *Thinking about Children*, Cambridge, Cambridge University Press.

Cadoret, R. J. *et al.* (1975) 'Studies of Adoptees from Psychiatrically Disturbed Biological Parents II', *The Journal of Paediatrics*, vol. 87, no. 2, pp. 301–6.

Cadoret, R. J. *et al.* (1976) 'Studies of Adoptees from Psychiatrically Disturbed Biological Parents', III, *American Journal of Psychiatry*, vol. 133, no. 11, pp. 1316–18.

Churchill, S. R. *et al.* (ed.) (1979) *No Child is Unadoptable*, London, Sage Publications.

Clarke, A. M. (1981) 'Adoption Studies', *Adoption and Fostering*, 104, pp. 17–29.

Clarke, A. M. and Clarke, A. D. B. (1976) *Early Experience: Myth and Evidence* London, Open Books.

Clothier, F. (1943) 'The Psychology of the Adopted Child', *Mental Hygiene*, vol. 27, pt. 2, pp. 222–30.

Cook, T. (1982) 'Listen to Your Clients', *Community Care*, 3.

Cooper, J. D. (1978) *Patterns of Family Placement*, London, National Children's Bureau.

Cunningham, L. *et al.* (1975) 'Studies of Adoptees from Psychiatrically Disturbed Biological Parents', *British Journal of Psychiatry*, 126, pp. 534–9.

Curtis, P. (1982) 'Communicating Through Play', *Adoption and Fostering*, vol. 6, no. 1, pp. 27–31.

Curtis, P. (1983) 'Involving Children in the Placement Process', *Adoption and Fostering*, vol. 7, no. 1, pp. 45–7.

Day, C. (1980) 'Access to Birth Records: General Register Office Study', in *Access to Birth Records*, London, BAAF, pp. 21–33.

d'Entreves, A. P. (1951) *Natural Law*, London, Hutchinson.

DHSS (1979) *Adoption Development Project: The First Year*, London, HMSO, limited circulation.

Dillow, L. B. (1968) 'The Group Process in Adoptive Home-Finding', *Children*, vol. 15, no. 4, pp. 153–7.

Donley, K. (1975) *Opening New Doors*, London, ABAFA.

Draper, J. (1978) 'When Social Services Abused a Family', *Community Care*, no. 242, pp. 4–5.

Eck Menning, B. (1977) *Infertility: a Guide for the Childless Couple*, New Jersey, Prentice Hall.

Edwards, A. M. (1975) 'The Use of a Self-Questionnaire for Psychiatric Screening of Prospective Adopters', *Child Adoption*, no. 82, pp. 42–4.

Eiduson, B. T. and Livermore, J. B. (1952) 'Complications in Therapy with Adopted Children', *Am. J. of Orthopsychiatry*, vol. 23, pp. 795–802.

Eldred, C. A. *et al.* (1976) 'Some Aspects of Adoption in Selected Samples of Adult Adoptees', *Am. J. of Orthopsychiatry*, vol. 46, no. 2, pp. 279–90.

Ellison, M. (1958) *The Adopted Child*, London, Victor Gollancz.

Elonen, A. and Schwartz, E. M. (1969) 'A Longitudinal Study of Emotional, Social and Academic Functioning of Adopted Children', *Child Welfare*, vol. 48, no. 2, pp. 72–8.

Erikson, R. E. (1961) 'Counselling After Legal Adoption', *Child Welfare*, vol. 40, pp. 21–5.

Fahlberg, V. (1981) *Helping Children when they Must Move*, London, BAAF.

Fahlberg, V. (1982) *Child Development*, London, BAAF.

Fanshel, D. (1962) 'Approaches to Measuring Adjustment in Adoptive Parents', in *Quantitative Approaches to Parent Selection*, New York, Child Welfare League of America, pp. 18–35.

Fanshel, D. (1972) *Far from the Reservation: The Transracial Adoption of American Indian Children*, Metuchen, N.J. Scarecrow Press.

Fanshel, D. and Shinn, E. (1978) *Children in Foster Care: A Longitudinal Study*, New York, Columbia UP.

Farber, S. (1977) 'Sex Differences in the Expression of Adoption Ideas', *Am. Journal of Orthopsychiatry*, vol. 47, no. 4, pp. 639–50.

Ferguson, H. K. (1981) 'Open Adoption', *Adoption and Fostering*, vol. 104, no. 2, pp. 45–7.

Fisch, R. O. *et al.* 'Growth, Behavioural and Psychologic Measurements of Adopted Children', *The Journal of Paediatrics*, vol. 89, no. 3, pp. 494–500.

Fitzgerald, J. (1983) *Understanding Disruption*, London, BAAF.

Fitzgerald, J. and James, M. (1981) 'Black Parents for Black Children', *Adoption and Fostering*, vol. 103, no. 1, pp. 10–17.

Fitzgerald, J. *et al.* (1982) *Building New Families*, Oxford, Blackwell.

Fox, L. M. (1982) 'Two Value Positions in Recent Child Care Law and Practice', *British J. of Social Work*, vol. 12, no. 3, pp. 265–90.

Freeman, M. D. A. (1981) 'Rights of Children in Care', in Rawstron, D. (ed.) *Rights of Children*, London, BAAF, pp. 5–18.

Freud, S. (1957) 'Family Romances', in *Collected Papers*, vol. 5, London, Hogarth Press.

Frisk, M. (1964) 'Identity Problems and Confused Conceptions of the Genetic Ego in Adopted Children During Adolescence', *Acta Paedopsychiatrica*, vol. 31, pp. 6–12.

Garn, S. M. *et al.* (1976) 'Similarities between Parents and their Adopted Children', *Am. Journal of Physical Anthropology*, 45, pp. 539–44.

George, V. (1970) *Foster Care: Theory and Practice*, London, Routledge & Kegan Paul.

Gill, O. and Jackson, B. (1982) 'Transracial Adoption in Britain', *Adoption and Fostering*, vol. 6, no. 3, pp. 30–5.

Gill, O. and Jackson, B. (1983) *Adoption and Race*, London, Batsford.

Gochros, H. L. (1967) 'A Study of the Caseworker – Adoptive Parent Relationship in Post-Placement Services', *Child Welfare*, vol. 46, no. 6, pp. 317–25.

Goldstein, J. *et al.* (1973) *Beyond the Best Interests of the Child*, London, Collier-Macmillan.

Goldstein, J. *et al.* (1980) *Before the Best Interests of the Child*, London, Burnett Books.

Goodman, J. D. *et al.* (1943) 'Adopted Children Brought to Child Psychiatric Clinics', *Archives of General Psychiatry*, vol 9, pp. 451–6.

Goodridge, C. (1975) 'Special Techniques in the Group Adoptive Study for Children with Special Needs', LIV, I, pp. 35–9.

Goodwin, D. W. *et al.* (1977) 'Alcoholism and Depression in Adopted-Out Daughters of Alcoholics', *Archives of General Psychiatry*, vol. 34, pp. 751–5.

Goodwin, D. W. *et al.* (1977) 'Psychopathology in Adopted and Non-Adopted Daughters of Alcoholics', *Archives of General Psychiatry*, pp. 1005–9.

Grey, E. and Blunden, R. M. (1971) *A Survey of Adoptions in Great Britain*, London, HMSO.

Grotevant, H. D. *et al.* (1977) 'Patterns of Interest Similarity in Adoptive Biological Families', *Journal of Personality and Social Psychology*, 35, 9, pp. 667–76.

Grow, L. J. and Shapiro, D. (1974) *Black Children, White Parents*, New York, Child Welfare League of America.

Hagen, C. H. (1972) *The Contribution of Social Work to Adoption*, Minnesota, Lutheran Social Service.

Hart, H. L. A. (1967) 'Are There Any Natural Rights?' in Quinton, A. (ed.) *Political Philosophy*, Oxford, Oxford University Press, pp. 53–67.

Hartman, A. (1979) *Finding Families*, London, Sage Publications.

Harvey, I. (1982) 'Transracial Adoption in Australia', *Adoption and Fostering*, vol. 6, no. 1, pp. 43–50.

Heim, A. (1982) *Thicker than Water: Adoption – its Loyalties, Pitfalls and Joys*, London, Secker & Warburg.

Holden, A. S. (1982) *Adoption '82*, Durham, Comyn Books.

Holman, R. (1973) *Trading in Children*, Routledge & Kegan Paul.

Holman, R. (1975) 'The Place of Fostering in Social Work', *British Journal of Social Work*, vol. 5, no. 1, pp. 3–30.

Holman, R. (1978) *Community Care*, 10.

Holman, R. (1976, 1980) *Inequality in Child Care*, CPAG.

Home Office and Scottish Home Department. (1954) *Report of the Departmental Committee on the Adoption of Children*, London, HMSO, Cmnd. 9248.

Home Office and Scottish Education Department. (1972) *Report of the Departmental Committee on the Adoption of Children*, London, HMSO, Cmnd. 5107.

Hoopes, J. L. *et al.* (1970) *A Follow-Up of Adoptions: Post Placement Functioning of Adopted Children*, vol. II, New York, Child Welfare League of America.

Horne, J. (1981) 'Groupwork with Adopters', *Adoption and Fostering*, vol. 106, no. 4, pp. 21–5.

Houghton, P. and Houghton, D. (1977) *Unfocused Grief: Responses to Childlessness*, Birmingham Settlement.

Humphrey, M. (1969) *The Hostage Seekers*, London, Longman.

Humphrey, M. and Ounstead, C. (1963) 'Adoptive Families Referred for Psychiatric Advice: Part I', *British Journal of Psychiatry*, vol. 109, pp. 599–608.

Hussell, C. and Monaghan, B. (1982) 'Going for Good', *Social Work Today*, vol. 13, no. 47, pp. 7–9.

Jacka, H. A. (1973) *Adoption in Brief*, NFER Publishing Company.

Jaffee, B. and Fanshel, D. (1970) *How They Fared in Adoption: A Follow-Up Study*, New York, Columbia University Press.

Jeffries, B. and Gillespie, A. (1981) 'Art Therapy with the Emotionally Frozen', *Adoption and Fostering*, vol. 106, no. 4, pp. 9–15.

Jenkins, R. (1969) 'Long Term Fostering', *Case Conference*, vol. 15, no. 9.

Jewett, C. (no date) *For Ever and Ever*, London, ABAFA.

Jewett, C. (1978) *Adopting the Older Child*, Harvard, Common Press.

Jonassohn, K. (1965) 'On the Use and Construction of Adoption Rates', *Journal of Marriage and Family Living*, vol. 27, no. 4, pp. 515.

Kadushin, A. (1966) 'Adoptive Parenthood: A Hazardous Adventure?' *Social Work*, vol. 11, pp. 30–9.

Kadushin, A. (1970a) *Adopting Older Children*, New York, Columbia University Press.

Kadushin, A. (1970b) 'Adoptive Status: Birth Parents v Bread Parents', *Child Care Quarterly Review*, vol. 14, no. 1, pp. 10–14.

Kadushin, A. (1972) *The Social Work Interview*, New York, Columbia University Press.

Kahan, B. (1979) *Growing Up in Care*, Oxford, Blackwell.

Karahasanoglu, A. *et al.* (1972) 'Psychological Aspects of Infertility', *The Journal of Reproductive Medicine*, vol. 9, no. 5, pp. 241–7.

Katz, L. (1979) 'Older Child Adoptive Placement: A Time of Family Crisis', in Churchill *et al.* (eds), *No Child is Unadoptable*, London, Sage Publications, pp. 95–101.

Kellmer-Pringle, M. L. (1961) 'The Incidence of Some Supposedly Adverse Family Conditions and of Left-Handedness in Schools for Maladjusted Children', *British Journal of Ed. Psychology*, vol. 31, pt. 2, pp. 183–93.

Kellmer-Pringle, M. L. (1967) *Adoption-Facts and Fallacies*, London, Longmans.

Kellmer-Pringle, M. L. (1975) *The Needs of Children*, London, Hutchinson.

Kerrane, A. (1979) 'Timing the Introduction', *Adoption and Fostering*, 96, pp. 23–5.

Kerrane, A. *et al.* (1980) *Adopting Older and Handicapped Children*, Essex, Dr Barnardo's.

Kirk, D. (1964) *Shared Fate*, London, Collier-Macmillan.

Kirk, D. (1970) 'The Selection of Adopters', *Medical Group Papers II: Genetic and Psychological Aspects of Adoption*, London, Assn. of British Adoption and Fostering Agencies.

Kirk, D. *et al.* (1966) 'Are Adopted Children More Vulnerable to Stress?' *Archives of General Psychiatry*, vol. 14, pp. 219–98.

Kohlsaat, B. and Johnson, A. M. (1954) 'Some Suggestions for Practice in Infant Adoption', *Social Casework*, vol. 35, pp. 91–9.

Kornitzer, M. (1968) *Adoption and Family Life*, London, Putnam.

Kornitzer, M. (1976) 'It Just So Happened', *Adoption and Fostering*, 58, pp. 21–9.

Krugman, D. C. 'Reality in Adoption', *Child Welfare*, vol. 43, pp. 349–58.

Kuhlmann, F. M. and Robinson, H. P. (1951) 'Rorschach Tests as a Diagnostic Tool in Adoption Studies', *Social Casework*, vol. 32, pp. 15–22.

Lambert, L. (1971) 'Adoption: The Statistical Picture, 1970', *Child Adoption*, no. 63, pp. 11–22.

Lambert, L. and Streather, S. (1980) *Children in Changing Families*, London, Macmillan.

Lambrick, H. (1974) 'Adoption as an Ordeal', *Child Adoption*, no. 78, pp. 63–7.

Lasson, I. (no date) *Where's My Mum*, Birmingham: Pepar Publications.

Lawder, E. *et al.* (1969) *A Follow-Up Study of Adoptions: Post Placement Functioning of Adoptive Families*, New York, Child Welfare League of America.

Leeding, A. (1980) 'Access to Birth Records: The Local Authority Experience', in *Access to Birth Records*, London, BAAF, pp. 9–20.

Lock, J. (1959) *An Essay Concerning Human Understanding*, New York, Dover Publications.

Lockridge, F. (1947) *Adopting a Child*, New York, Greenberg.

McKay, M. (1980) 'Planning for Permanent Placement', *Adoption and Fostering*, 99, pp. 19–21.

MacKay, S. J. (1982) *Making Decisions in Adoption*, Edinburgh, Family Care.

McWhinnie, A. M. (1967) *Adopted Children: How They Grow Up*, London, Routledge & Kegan Paul.

Mai, F. M. (1971) 'Conception after Adoption: An Open Question', *Psychosomatic Medicine*, vol. 33, no. 6, pp. 509–14.

Mai, F. M. *et al.* (1972a) 'Psychiatric Interview Comparisons Between Infertile and Fertile Couples', *Psychosomatic Medicine*, vol. 34, no. 5, pp. 431–40.

Mai, F. M. *et al.* (1972b) 'Psychosomatic and Behavioural Mechanisms in Psychogenic Infertility', *British Journal of Psychiatry*, vol. 120, pp. 199–204.

Mann, P. (1977) 'Working with Children', *Adoption and Fostering*, 89, pp. 42–5.

Martin, H. (1976) *The Abused Child*, Cambridge, Mass., Ballinger.

Mayer, J. and Timms, N. (1970) *The Client Speaks*, London, Routledge & Kegan Paul.

Menlove, F. L. (1965) 'Aggressive Symptoms in Emotionally Disturbed Adopted Children', *Child Development*, vol. 36, pp. 519–32.

Middlestadt, E. (1978) 'Using Adoptive Parents', *Adoption and Fostering*, 93, pp. 18–22.

Morrison, J. R. and Stewart, M. A. (1973) 'The Psychiatric Status of the Legal Families of Adopted Hyperactive Children', *Archives of General Psychiatry*, vol. 28, pp. 888–91.

Napier, H. (1972) 'Success and Failure in Foster Care', *British Journal of Social Work*, vol. 2, no. 2.

Natanson, M. (1970) *The Journeying Self*, London, Addison-Wesley.

National Children's Bureau. (1983) *Highlight*, no. 56.

National Assn. for Mental Health. (1953) *A Survey Based on Adoption Case Records*, London, NAMH.

Neilson, J. (1979) 'Placing Children in Adoptive Homes: Excerpts', in Churchill *et al.* (eds), *No Child is Unadoptable*, London, Sage Publications, pp. 84–101.

Offord, D. R. *et al.* (1969) 'Presenting Symptomatology of Adopted Children', *Archives of General Psychiatry*, vol. 20, no. 1, pp. 110–16.

Packman, J. (1975) *The Child's Generation*, London, Martin Robinson.

Page, R. and Clark, G. A. (eds) (1979) *Who Cares?* London, National Children's Bureau.

Palmer, T. (1973) 'Matching Worker and Client in Connections', *Social Work*, vol. 18, pp. 95–103.

Parker, R. (1966) *Decision in Childcare*, London, Allen & Unwin.

Parker, R. (1971) *Planning for Deprived Children*, London, National Children's Home.

Parker, R. A. (ed.) (1980) *Caring for Separated Children*, London, Macmillan.

Peller, L. (1961) 'About Telling the Child of His Adoption', *Bulletin of the Phil. Assn. for Psycho-Analysis*, vol. 11, pp. 145–54.

Picton, C. and Seagar, M. (1977) 'Post Adoption', *Adoption and Fostering*, 88, pp. 21–9.

Pilling, D. and Kellmer-Pringle, M. (1978) *Controversial Issues in Child Development*, London, Paul Elek.

Platt, J. J. *et al.* (1973) 'Infertile Couples: Personality Traits and Self-Ideal Concept Discrepancies', *Fertility and Sterility*, vol. 24, pp. 972–6.

Prosser, H. (1976) *Perspectives on Residential Child Care*, NFER.

Prosser, H. (1978) *Perspectives on Foster Care*, NFER.

Raleigh, B. (1954) 'Adoption as a Factor in Child Guidance', *Smith College Studies in Social Work*, vol. 25, pp. 53–71.

Rawstron, D. (1980) *Child Care Law*, London, BAAF.

Raynor, L. (1970) *Adoption of Non-White Children*, London, Allen & Unwin.

Raynor, L. (1980) *The Adopted Child Comes of Age*, London, Allen & Unwin.

Reece, S. A. and Levin, B. (1968) 'Psychiatric Disturbances in Adopted Children', *Social Work*, vol. 13, no. 1, pp. 101–11.

Reeves, S. and Dolan, P. (1978) 'A Retrospective Assessment of Adoption', *Clearing House for Local Authority Social Services Research*, no. 8, pp. 83–126.

Reid, J. (1973) 'Group Meetings for Adoption Applicants', *Child Adoption*, no. 74, pp. 41–3.

Renne, D. (1977) 'There's Always Adoption', *Child Welfare*, vol. 56, pp. 465–70.

Report of the Steering Group. (1977) *The Soul Kids Campaign*, London, ABAFA.

Richards, K. (1970) 'The Social Worker's View', *Medical Group Papers II: Genetic and Psychological Aspects of Adoption*, London, British Agencies for Adoption and Fostering, pp. 68–76.

Ringwood, P. (1976) 'Adoption Procedures in the Cook Islands and New Zealand', *Adoption and Fostering*, 85, pp. 47–52.

Ripple, L. (1968) 'A Follow-Up Study of Adopted Children', *Social Services Review*, vol. 42, no. 4, pp. 479–99.

Rock, J. *et al.* (1965) 'Effects of Adoption on Infertility', *Fertility and Sterility*, vol. 16, no. 3, pp. 305–12.

Rosenthal, D. *et al.* (1975) 'Parent–Child Relationships and Psychopathological Disorders in the Child', *Archives of General Psychiatry*, vol. 32, pp. 466–76.

Rosner, G. (1961) *Crisis of Self Doubt*, New York, Child Welfare League of America.

Rothenberg, E. W. *et al.* (1971) 'The Vicissitudes of the Adoption Process', *Am. Journal of Psych.*, vol. 128, no. 5, pp. 590–5.

Rowe, J. (1966) *Parents, Children and Adoption*, London, Routledge & Kegan Paul.

Rowe, J. (1971) 'The Reality of the Adoptive Family', in Tod, R. (ed.) *Social Work in Adoption*, London, Longman, pp. 144–54.

Rowe, J. and Lambert, L. (1973) *Children Who Wait*, London, Assn. of British Adoption and Fostering Agencies.

Rutter, M. (1970) 'Psychological Development – Predictions from Infancy', *Journal of Child Psychology and Psychiatry*, vol. II, No. 1, pp. 49–62.

Rutter, M. (1981) *Maternal Deprivation Reassessed*, 2nd ed., Harmondsworth, Penguin Books.

Ryan, T. and Walker, R. (1983) *Making Life Story Books*, privately published.

Sandler, B. (1961) 'Infertility of Emotional Origin', *Journal of Obstetrics and Gynaecology – Gt. Britain*, vol. 68, pp. 809–15.

Sants, H. J. (1977) 'Genealogical Bewilderment in Children with Substitute Parents', in *Child Adoption*, London, BAAF, pp. 67–77.

Sawbridge, P. (1978) 'Homes for the Hardest to Place', *Adoption and Fostering*, 93, pp. 13–18.

Schechter, M. D. (1960) 'Observations on Adopted Children', *Archives of General Psychiatry*, vol. 3, pp. 45/21–56/32.

Schechter, M. D. *et al.* (1964) 'Emotional Problems in the Adoptee', *Archives of General Psychiatry*, vol. 10, pp. 109–18.

Schorr, A. (1978) quoted by R. Holman in 'A Class Analysis of Adoption Reveals a Disturbing Picture', *Community Care*, 26 April, p. 13.

Schroeder, H. and Lightfoot, D. (1983) 'Finding Black Families', *Adoption and Fostering*, vol. 7, no. 1, pp. 18–22.

Schwartz, E. M. (1970) 'The Family Romance Fantasy in Children Adopted in Infancy', *Child Welfare*, vol. XLIX, no. 7, pp. 386–91.

Seglow, J. *et al.* (1972) *Growing Up Adopted*, NFER Publishing Company.

Sensel, B. and Yeakel, M. (1970) 'Relationship Capacity and Acknowledgement of Difference in Adoptive Parenthood', *Smith College Studies in Social Work*, vol. 40, no. 2, pp. 155–63.

Seward, G. H. *et al.* (1965) 'The Question of Psychophysiologic Infertility', *Psycho-Somatic Medicine*, vol. 27, no. 6, pp. 533–44.

Shaw, L. A. (1953) 'Following-Up Adoptions', *British Journal of Psychiatric Social Work*, vol. 8, pp. 14–21.

Shaw, M. and Hiprave, T. (1982) 'Specialist Fostering: A Review of the Current Scene', *Adoption and Fostering* 6, 4, pp. 21–5.

Shaw, M. and Lebens, K. (1978) *What Shall we do with the Children?* London, BAAF.

Shaw, M. *et al.* (1975) *Children Between Families*, Leicester, University School of Social Work.

Short, R. and Gray, G. (1982) 'Foster Parents Must be Trained', *Community Care*, pp. 14–16.

Simms, M. and Smith, C. (1982) 'Teenage Mothers and Adoption', *Adoption and Fostering*, vol. 6, no. 4, pp. 43–8.

Simon, J. R. and Altstein, H. (1977) *Transracial Adoption*, London, John Wiley.

Simon, J. R. and Alstein, H. (1981) *Transracial Adoption: A Follow-Up*, Lexington Books.

Simon, N. D. and Senturia, A. G. (1966) 'Adoption and Psychiatric Illness', *Am. J. of Psych.*, vol. 122, pp. 858–68.

Singleton, R. (1979) 'Appealing Against Case Committees', *Adoption and Fostering*, 96, pp. 43–4.

Skodak, M. and Skeels, H. M. (1949) 'A Final Follow-Up Study of One Hundred Adopted Children', *The Journal of Genetic Psychology*, vol. 75, pp. 85–125.

Smith, C. R. (1980) *Adoption Policy and Practice* (University of Leeds: Ph.D. Thesis).

Soothill, K. (1982) 'Foster Parents: The Use of a Resource', *British Journal of Social Work*, 12, pp. 92–5.

Soothill, K. and Derbyshire, M. (1981) 'Selecting Foster Parents', *Adoption and Fostering*, 104, pp. 47–50.

Sorosky, A. D. *et al.* (1975) 'Identity Conflicts in Adoption', *Am. Journal of Orthopsychiatry*, vol. 45, no. 1, pp. 18–27.

Sweeny, D. *et al.* (1963) 'A Descriptive Study of Adopted Children Seen in a Child Guidance Centre', *Child Welfare*, vol. 42, pp. 345–9.

Tessler, R. C. (1975) 'Clients' Reactions to Initial Interviews', *Journal of Counselling Psychology*, vol. 22, no. 3, pp. 187–91.

Thorpe, R. (1974) 'Mum and Mrs So and So', *Social Work Today*, vol. 4, no. 22.

Thunen, M. (1958) 'Ending Contact with Adoptive Parents: The Group Meeting', *Child Welfare*, vol. 37, 8–14.

Timms, N. (1973) *The Receiving End*, London, Routledge & Kegan Paul.

Timms, N. and Timms, R. (1977) *Perspectives in Social Work*, London, Routledge & Kegan Paul.

Tizard, B. (1977) *Adoption: A Second Chance*, London, Open Books.

Todd, R. (ed.) (1971) *Social Work in Adoption*, London, Longman.

Toussieng, P. W. (1962) 'Thoughts Regarding the Etiology of Psychological Difficulties in Adopted Children', *Child Welfare*, vol. 41, pp. 59–65.

Toussieng, P. W. (1971) 'Realising the Potential in Adoptions', *Child Welfare*, vol. L., no. 6, pp. 322–7.

Trasler, G. (1960) *In Place of Parents*, London, Routledge & Kegan Paul.

Triseliotis, J. P. (1970) *Evaluation of Adoption Policy and Practice*, Edinburgh University.

Triseliotis, J. P. (1973) *In Search of Origins*, London, Routledge & Kegan Paul.

Triseliotis, J. P. (1978) 'Growing Up Fostered', *Adoption and Fostering*, vol. 94, no. 4, pp. 11–24.

Triseliotis, J. P. (ed.) (1980) *New Developments in Foster Care and Adoption*, London, Routledge & Kegan Paul.

Triseliotis, J. P. (1983) 'Identity and Security in Adoption and Long Term Fostering', *Adoption and Fostering*, vol. 7, no. 1, pp. 22–31.

Triseliotis, J. P. and Lobban, V. (1973) 'Recent Developments Affecting Adoption Numbers and Adoption Practice', *British Journal of Social Work*, vol. 5, no. 3, pp. 333–4.

Unger, C. *et al.* (1977) *Chaos, Madness and Unpredictability: Placing the Child with Ears Like Uncle Harry's*, Michigan, Spaulding for Children.

Waters, W. H. R. (1977) 'The GP and Sub-Fertility', *Child Adoption*, London, ABAFA, pp. 158–62.

Weinstein, E. A. (1962) 'Adoption and Infertility', *American Sociological Review*, 27, pp. 408–12.

Weinstein, R. (1960) *The Self-Image of the Foster Child*, New York, Russell Sage Foundation.

Weir, W. E. and Weir, D. R. (1966) 'Adoption and Subsequent Conception', *Fertility and Sterility*, vol. 17, no. 2, pp. 283–8.

White, R. (1980) 'A Legal View', in Adcock *et al.* (eds), *Terminating Parental Contact*, London, BAAF, pp. 6–13.

White, R. (1982) 'Wardship Proceedings', *Adoption and Fostering*, vol. 6, no. 3, pp. 40–7.

Wieder, H. (1977) 'The Family Romance Fantasies of Adopted Children', *Psycho-Analytical Quarterly*, vol. 46, no. 2, pp. 155–200.

Wiehe, V. R. (1972) 'The Group Adoptive Study', *Child Welfare*, vol. 51, no. 10, pp. 645–9.

Wiehe, V. R. (1976) 'Attitudinal Change as a Function of the Adoptive Study', *Smith College Studies in Social Work*, vol. 46, pp. 127–36.

Witmer, H. L. *et al.* (1963) *Independent Adoptions*, New York, Russell Sage Foundation.

Wittenborn, J. R. (1957) *The Placement of Adoptive Children*, Illinois, Charles C. Thomas.

Work, H. H. and Anderson, H. (1971) 'Studies in Adoption', *American Journal of Psychiatry*, vol. 127, no. 7, pp. 948–50.

Working Party on Fostering Practice (1976) *A Guide to Fostering Practice*, London, HMSO.

Zur Nieden, M. (1951) 'The Influence of Constitution and Environment upon the Development of Adopted Children', *Journal of Psychology*, 31, pp. 91–5.

Index